First Strokes

Kayak Touring For Sit-on-Top and Sit-Inside Kayaks

by Mitch Powers

Mariposa Publishing

Mariposa Publishing

Greenbrae, CA
Printed in USA
3rd Edition

Copyright 2012 by Mitch Powers

Written by Mitch Powers
Photography by Mitch Powers & Michael Morgan
Cover Design by Roger Knox
General Layout by Mitch Powers
Email: Positiveoutlook1@hotmail.com

Contents

Introduction..IV

Chapter 1: Starting Off...1
    Sit-on-top vs. Sit-inside Kayak..........................2
    Basic Kayak Clothing.......................................11
    Outfitting your Kayak......................................13

Chapter 2: Paddle Strokes...19
    Paddle Types...19
    Forward Stroke..24
    Sweep Strokes..29
    Draw Strokes...33
    Bracing Strokes...36

Chapter 3: Rescues for Sit-on-Tops..............................45
    Self-rescue...46
    Assisted Rescue...49
    Double Rescue..50

Chapter 4: Rescues for Sit-Insides..............................53
    Paddle Float Rescue.......................................53
    Alternative Single Recues................................63
    T-Rescue...66
    Doubles Rescue..68

Chapter 5: Storage, Transportation, Launching, Practice.........77
    Kayak Storage..77
    Transporting Your Kayak...................................79
    Launching..82
    Practicing Skills on the Water..........................89

Chapter 6: Trip Planning and Safety.............................99
    Trip Planning Checklist...................................99
    Weather, Tides and Currents............................101
    Communication Signals....................................104
    Safety and Judgement......................................107
    Ranging..108
    Progressing to the Next Level..........................110

Introduction

People have incredible responses to gliding across the water in a kayak. Most notably it's the intimate connection to nature that it offers. As your kayaking experience evolves you will experience more and more this connection whether you are paddling local or distant waters.

First Strokes is intended to bring you to this place by teaching basic through intermediate skills for those paddling sit-on-top or sit-inside kayaks. I've included both types of kayak in this book because they each offer an excellent way to get out on the water. Also, there is a lot of cross over between the two types of watercraft. For example, all the paddling strokes are the same. And when traveling, especially in warmer climates, sit-inside type kayakers often find themselves renting sit-on-tops. Why not be comfortable paddling both types of craft to explore your world?

It doesn't matter whether you are a recreational type paddler or someone intent on pursuing advanced paddling skills, this book will take you from A-Z covering all the nuts and bolts of kayaking. With this background you will enjoy your kayaking experience more while keeping it safe.

A word on how this tome is organized. The first chapter starts out discussing basic kayaking equipment. The next chapters cover paddle strokes and rescues, and then we get into launching a kayak and practice sessions on the water. This is followed by a trip planning section geared towards safety on the water. Where appropriate, throughout the chapters, I have created separate sections specific to either sit-on-top or sit-inside kayak equipment and skills.

First Strokes will take you well beyond introductory skill levels. You will find at the end of the paddle stroke and rescue chapters sections on "common problems" and "practice sessions" to help you fine tune your skills. Additionally, there are sections including: doubles rescues, basics of reading a tidelog, navigational tools, a trip planning checklist and a step by step approach for those wishing to progress to an "advanced" kayaking skill level.

Since this book is more for day trippers than those planning a National Geographic style outing to the artic it doesn't get into some of the more esoteric aspects of the boating experience. I have not included anything on compass navigation, chart reading or use of a GPS. The fact is, most paddlers never use any of these tools. Most of us just want to get out on the water, paddle, enjoy nature, and bag some exercise. First Strokes also doesn't cover more advanced skills like the roll, and surf launches/landings.

Remember, the best safety device you'll ever have while paddling is your brain. That said, taking kayaking classes as a compliment to using this book is a great idea. There's nothing like the personal touch of a seasoned instructor to help you along the road of refining technique and promoting safety on the water.

And soon enough you'll be out there gliding along.

Chapter 1: Starting Off

In this chapter we'll discuss kayak types and designs, gear, clothing and "outfitting" your boat.

Keep in mind that there is an incredible amount of choices today in terms of different kayak designs and related gear. After all, kayaking is a fast growing sport. As a beginner, purchasing a kayak and all the companion gear should not be on your radar screen. Give yourself a little time to understand the various choices and to determine what is best for you. Get out and test out different boats. How can you do this if you don't have the basic gear? Generally, kayak outfitters that rent kayaks and teach classes have gear and clothing for use such as PFD's (lifejackets), wetsuits and paddle jackets. If not, see what you can borrow from friends or dig up in the garage.

After renting from an outfitter, taking classes, using friends kayaks, or checking out boat demo days sponsored by your local outfitters, you'll be able to make more informed purchase decisions. Remember, while you may feel overwhelmed with all the new skills being learned and variety of equipment choices, the learning curve is quite rapid. Just get in there and get your feet wet. And soon you'll be paddling your way to adventure!

KAYAKING TYPES: SIT-ON-TOP VS. SIT-INSIDE KAYAKS

The Kayak

What defines a kayak versus other types of human powered watercraft? Firstly, kayakers use a double bladed paddle unlike canoeists or outrigger paddlers that use a single bladed paddle. And of course, unlike individual rowers who use two oars and travel backwards, kayakers are always moving forward.

The sit-on-top kayak is fairly self-explanatory. There is no cockpit and the paddler simply sits in a molded seat best outfitted with a seat pad and backrest. On sit-on-top's the whole body is exposed to the elements versus sit-inside kayaks which are decked boats where your legs run inside the kayak. The opening or cockpit of the sit-inside kayak is sealed off with a sprayskirt. The sprayskirt in turn keeps water from entering your cockpit and hence flooding the boat. This also keeps your lower half protected against the elements.

What's in a name? The name sit-on-top kayak is universally understood and refers to recreational type sit-on-top kayaks. Sit-inside kayaks however are also sometimes referred to as sea kayaks, traditional sea kayaks, traditional kayaks, or touring kayaks. The very term sea kayak and sea kayaking, which conjures up images of adventures in the wild, rugged coastlines and expedition style trips to offshore islands, might be a bit misleading if not downright intimidating. The majority of sea kayakers or sit-inside kayakers are mostly interested in "kayak touring" on relatively calm bodies of water like flat rivers, ponds, lakes, bays and estuaries. Most sit-on-top kayakers are also looking for a similar experience.

Kayak Design

Typically kayaks are constructed of either polyethylene (plastic), or composites like fiberglass or Kevlar and carbon. There is also a newer technology for making kayaks called "thermoform". Thermoformed kayaks in terms of quality, weight and price form a compromise between the less expensive plastic or "tupperware" boats and the more pricey, higher performance and lighter composite boats. The exceptions to these materials are in wooden and folding kayaks.

Most recreational sit-on-top kayaks tend to be made of plastics, and hence are heavier and tend to flex more than glass boats of the same relative size. Fiberglass kayaks, being stiffer and lighter, offer greater performance than plastic boats but

2

when you're really feeling plush with cash go for kevlar or a combination of kevlar and carbon for lightness and strength. In the interim plastic works just fine and the big difference is in the pocketbook!

Before purchasing a kayak, as I said before, it makes sense to try different models out and of course to answer that all important question: sit-on-top or sit-inside? Eventually in your kayaking experience you'll probably paddle both depending on where you are, what's available and your expectations. But for now here are a few thoughts to help you decide what's best for you to start out on.

Firstly, most outfitters will let you rent a sit-on-top kayak without a half day or all day formal class. They'll give you the basics, discuss boundaries, safety issues and away you go. On the other hand most responsible outfitters require you take a rescue class or know your basic rescues to rent sit-inside kayaks. Why? When they flip they fill up with water and the self-rescue is a bit more tricky. If you are traveling to warm climates, generally what's available to rent or for guided tours are sit-on-top kayaks. Sometimes the choice comes down to your local weather patterns. If you live in a colder more rainy climate a sit-inside kayak will keep you warmer and dryer. Sit-inside kayaks in general tend to be higher performance kayaks in terms of boat handling and speed. They also tend to be a better choice for things like kayak camping and surf launches and landings. That said there are many sit-on-top kayaks that are faster and more agile than many poke about recreational sit-inside kayaks.

Some people prefer the simplicity of sit-on-top kayaks. Plop your butt in the seat and go. There are also those that have an anxiety of being trapped in their sit-inside kayak should they flip. The thing to do is try both types of kayak and see what works best for you. Just remember, if you get on the track of becoming a more advanced kayaker, eventually you'll be looking for a higher performance boat.

Anatomy of a Kayak

Kayaks come in a dazzling variety of lengths, widths, hull shapes and design particulars that offer different performance characteristics. It's not within the scope of this book to make you an expert on boat designs and choices but there are some basics to be aware of to help you start understanding the difference in kayak types.

The speed of a kayak and its handling qualities is directly related to its length, width, weight, hull shape and of course you the paddler. The most efficient (fastest) kayaks are light, long, narrow and have rounded hulls. But a kayak like this is also

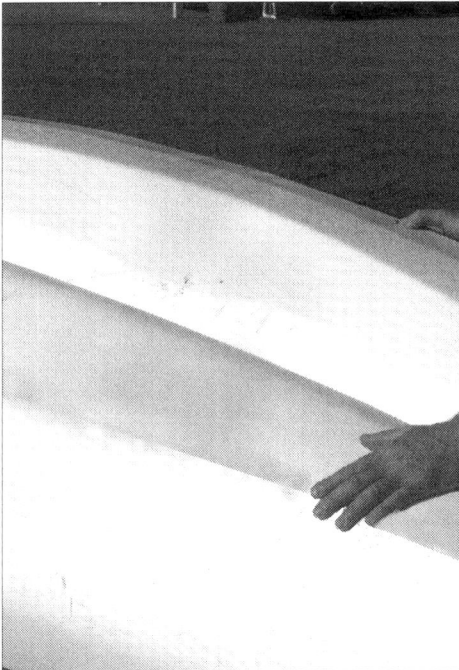

| See rounder edge on the lower sit-inside and the cut or chined edge on the upper boat. | Sit-on-top hull: a roundish keel flattening out to the sides and four scuppers (draining holes). |

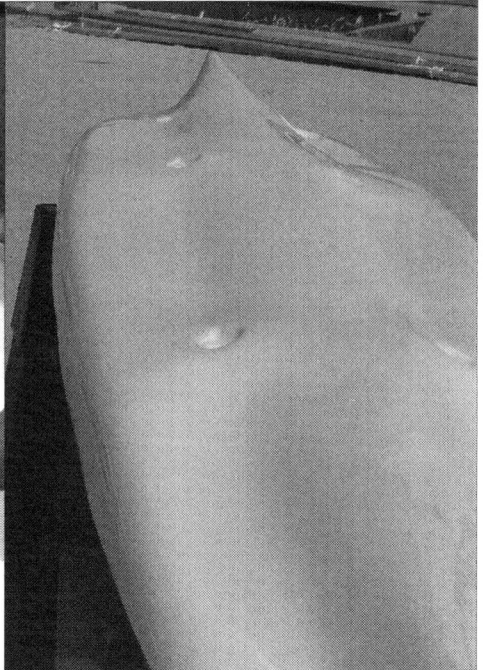

very tippy, hard to handle in chop and not appropriate for the recreational paddler. A short, wide and more flat bottomed kayak is easier to turn, and provides for a very stable platform. Somewhere in between these two kayaks is the one you'll most likely want to paddle.

Hull shapes can be flat, v-shaped, chined or a hybrid of the above. In evaluating the choices several questions come to mind. What's the primary stability of the kayak like? In other words when your kayak is level to the surface of the water how stable is it for you? What about the secondary stability? That is, how hard or easy is it to lean the kayak on its edge and maintain that lean? In conjunction with these questions is another: how easy is the boat to turn? Kayaks with flat hulls tend to turn easily but usually offer little secondary stability. A rounded hull has neither good primary or secondary stability and doesn't turn especially easily. This begs the question what good is a rounded hull? This is best answered by asking any kayaking racer and don't forget to bring a six pac because you're in for a long discussion.

If you plan on just poking around a harbor and paddling minimal distances, a

4

shorter kayak has advantages because of the lighter weight, responsive turning and its easier to lift up on a car. Here, speed, time and distance are not an issue. You are a casual recreational paddler and you have no desire to paddle in windy, choppy or high current conditions. Anything that gets you on the water is good. Rudder or no rudder no big deal.

Generally speaking, if you're planning on kayak touring where you travel distances of four miles and up and might be exposed to some chop and wind you'll want a kayak that is a bit longer and either tracks well or has a drop down rudder. Look for something that's 12-17 ½ feet long. If it's a sit-on-top the width will probably be 26-35 inches while a good sit-inside width range would be 22.5-25 inches. Keep in mind, when we talk about a kayaks width, that refers to the widest point. Stability is in part related to the width of a kayak and hull shape but also to the size of a paddler. A tall person with a well-developed upper body is going to have a higher center of gravity and hence its tends to be those big brawny guys that flop over first.

Fortunately, most kayaks are and should be a compromise suitable for all around conditions. So you might have a sit-on-top kayak that's 13-15 feet long, 26 inches wide and although it doesn't have a drop down rudder it does have a keel line that helps the boat track in light winds. Or you might have a sit-inside kayak that's 15 ½-17 ½ feet long and 23 inches wide with a very gentle v-shaped hull flattening out towards rounded edges which flair up to a chine. Wow!

Besides looking at the material, length, width and the hull shape, there's a few other typical considerations. How much rocker does your kayak have? This of course is related to hull shape at the bow (front) and stern (back) ends. The degree of rocker a kayak has refers to how upswept the bow and stern are. The more rocker a kayak has the easier it is to turn, and the harder it is to track straight without the use of a rudder, and the slower it is in flat water. A nicely rockered boat does well in chop and waves because instead of plowing into small waves and thus stalling it rises over the water. However, if you aren't using a rudder or your rudder breaks during a outing a highly rockered boat is a challenge to keep in a straight line even in small wind and wave conditions. The conclusion is that if you are poking around the harbor or lakeshore and just paddling short distances, like I said just about any type of kayak can work. However, if you're touring and covering more distance you'll want a boat to either have some natural tracking abilities or a rudder. Keep in mind some sit-inside kayaks use a drop down skeg system which provides great tracking (going in a straight line).

| 1. Traditional rudder in upright position controlled by a looped line running near the paddlers seated position. | 2. Skeg rudder system operated by a slider mechanism generally located to the side of the seated position. |

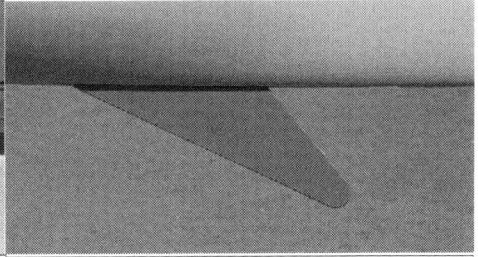

So what's it to be? Rudder or no rudder? Purists have their arguments against using a kayak with a rudder. It's one more thing that can break on a boat. And what if it breaks on a windy crossing and you are reliant on the rudder to control your boat. Now you've got a problem and a boat you can't control. So purists tend to go rudderless through life but hedge their bets with kayaks that have a keel line or a drop down skeg which both help the boat track straight.

Without getting sucked into the "Great Debate" any further, once again, the word compromise comes into mind. Eventually, when you buy a kayak, get one that has some built in tracking ability when the rudder is up. But buy a kayak with a rudder. Kayaks go to weather which means in a cross wind or even a slight breeze they turn into the wind. Imagine paddling a couple miles in a cross wind and your kayak constantly wants to turn and wander off course. And all the time you have to make compensatory strokes. Tiring and frustrating. Plop the rudder down and focus on a nice strong forward stroke, let your feet do the steering and watch those purists fall behind. But that said, a bow to the purists. It's extremely important that you practice controlling your kayak in wind and chop without using your rudder. So if you find that you are suddenly rudderless you will still have direction.

What else? If you have a sit-inside kayak, either for poking about or longer journeys it's a good idea to have flotation in the front and back or what are called sealed bulkheads. What if you take on water? What if you capsize? Flotation often comes in the form of blow up air bags or foam blocks. Most higher performance sit-inside kayaks nowadays have bulkheads where the front and rear compartments are sealed off. Your kayak won't sink if you flip or take on water. Not a bad concept. Bulkheads also provide support and stiffness to the kayak. If a sit-inside kayak doesn't have bulkheads it is probably an old boat or a cheap one. Either way you need to at least install air bags to provide flotation.

There's a dazzling array of different ways that the decks of kayaks are outfitted but basically you need secure deck rigging to stow things like your safety equipment, a deck bag, a water bottle and so forth. We'll talk about things to have with you in terms of safety on the water in a later chapter.

Kayak Terminology for sit-on-top and sit-inside kayaks

Get to know the various parts of your kayak so you'll have a common language to speak with other paddlers. Review the basic list below with names and descriptions and refer to the illustration.

Bow: Refers to the front end of the kayak.

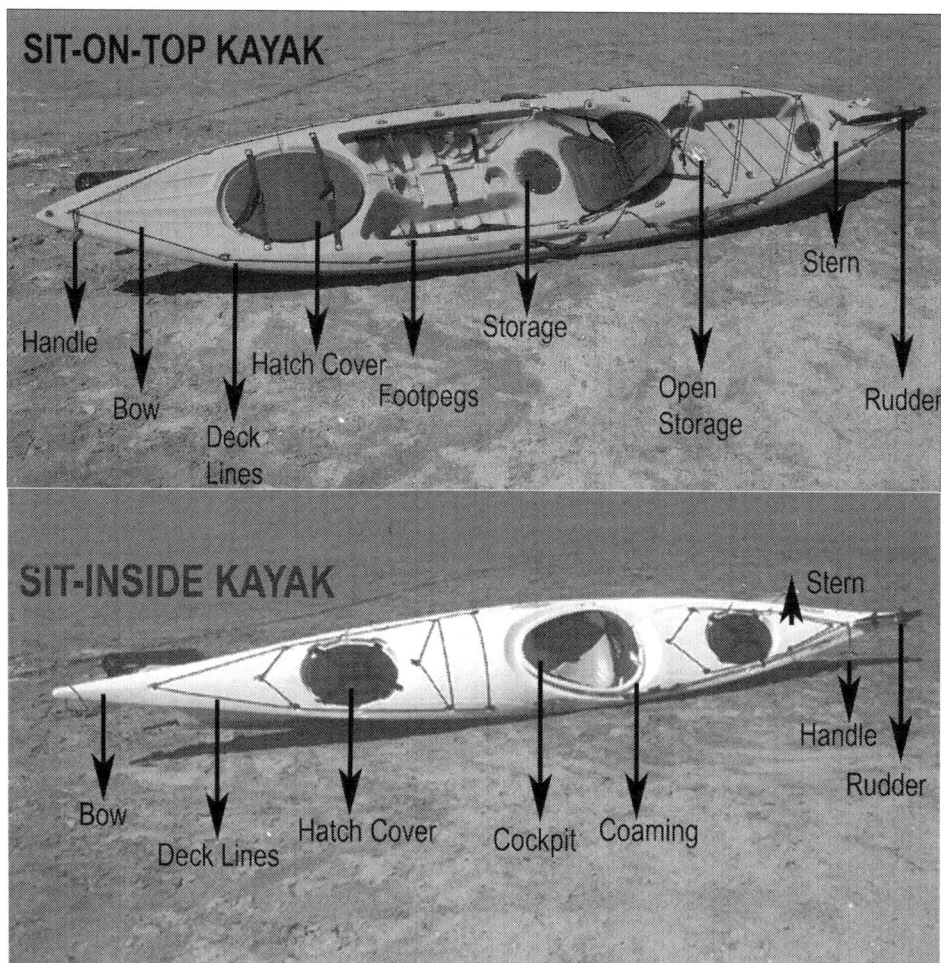

SIT-ON-TOP KAYAK

Handle
Bow
Hatch Cover
Deck Lines
Footpegs
Storage
Open Storage
Stern
Rudder

SIT-INSIDE KAYAK

Bow
Deck Lines
Hatch Cover
Cockpit
Coaming
Stern
Handle
Rudder

Stern: Refers to the rear end of the kayak.

Carrying Handles: Most kayaks have a handle or toggle near the bow and stern of the kayak for lifting and carrying the boat. Sometimes these are also referred to as grab loops.

Bow Hatch: This is the protective hard shell that covers the opening to the bow storage compartment where you pack gear. The bow hatch is held in place with straps and usually either has a built in seal (gasket) underneath, to provide a water tight fit, or there is a neoprene skirt cover that keeps the water out. Keep in mind not all kayaks have storage compartments.

Deck Lines: Usually made out of line and found around the deck perimeter of the kayak. Deck lines give paddlers another way to grab onto a kayak especially if they find themselves in the water.

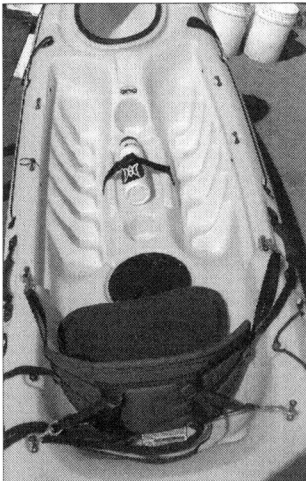

Deck Rigging: Made out of bungee cord and used to hold safety gear, water bottle etc.

Footwells and footpegs: Different kayaks different foot rest systems. Most sit-on-top kayaks which don't include rudders have footwells that are molded into the boat. Double sit-on-tops with rudders, which are controlled from the rear position, have footwells for the front paddler and footpegs for the rear position. The footpegs are adjustable and are attached to a track which slides in a bracket so your feet can control the rudder. Sit-inside kayaks have adjustable footpegs positioned inside the cockpit on tracks against the interior sidewalls of the kayak. In a rudderless sit-inside kayak, once the footpegs are adjusted they remain stationary, whereas if your kayak has a rudder and you are using it the footpegs (attached to the rudder via a cable) slide in a bracket the same as for sit-on-tops.

Cockpit: Refers to the opening in which a paddler slides into their sit-inside kayak

Coaming: This is the lip that surrounds the cockpit around which a sprayskirt fits for sit-inside kayaks.

8

| Sit-on-top with thigh straps | Adjustable sit-on-top seat |

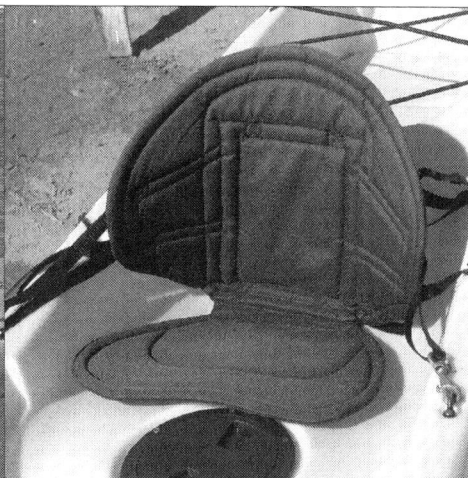

Thigh straps and thigh braces: Many sit-on-top kayaks can be rigged with thigh straps for greater boat control. These straps grab your thighs near the knee and allow you to edge (lean) your kayak, brace the boat in rougher conditions and in some cases even perform an roll. Sit-inside kayaks generally allow for much greater boat control as your legs can lock into the thigh brace areas under the deck of the boat.

Seat: Ideally your seat will have a seatback that is adjustable. Sometimes for comfort, kayakers customize their seats with a thin closed cell foam pad to sit on if not already included. The same type of customizing can be done with sit-inside kayaks for your thigh and hip contact points for comfort and tighter boat control.

Stern Hatch: This is the protective hard shell that covers the opening to the stern storage compartment where you pack gear. The stern hatch is held in place with straps and either has a built in seal underneath to provide a water tight fit or there is a neoprene skirt cover that keeps the water out. Generally, the stern storage compartment offers more storage room than the bow storage compartment.

Rudder: The variety is endless and not all kayaks come with a rudder system. Typically the rudder is lifted and dropped via lines that run up to a reachable position just behind the paddler's seated position. Boats with skeg type rudders, generally only sit-insides, have a lever/slide system reachable from the seated position.

Bulkheads: Bulkheads, found in sit-inside kayaks, seal off the bow and stern storage compartments providing both for buoyancy and dry gear. Cheaper recreational style sit-inside kayaks often are manufactured without bulkheads. They can be outfitted with flotation bags.

General Kayaking Gear

Along with your sit-on-top or sit-inside kayak, as a beginner there is some basic equipment you'll need each time you go paddling.

Kayak paddle: This is a double bladed paddle unlike a single bladed paddle used for canoes. See Chapter Two for details on different paddle types and lengths.

Water bottle: I've included this as a basic piece of equipment because as in any sport it's important to hydrate, hydrate, hydrate.

Drybag: Just as it implies a drybag is intended to keep those extra layers or that

camera dry. You'll probably buy one early in your kayaking experience and they come in a variety of sizes, shapes and colors. The clear ones are pretty neat because you can actually see where your stuffs positioned in the bag for easier access.

Other safety gear: We'll talk about additional safety gear such as towing systems (Chapter 5) and VHF radios and flares etc. in Chapter 6.

Kayak Gear Unique to Sit-inside Kayaks

Sprayskirt: Also, sometimes called a spraydeck. This is the piece of equipment worn around your waist which in turn seals around the kayak's cockpit coaming to keep water out. Most outfitters use a coated nylon type sprayskirt that comes with suspenders. Neoprene sprayskirts, if correctly sized, have a much tighter fit around the coaming and around a paddlers waist. This means a neoprene skirt is less likely to "blow out" when hit by a dumping wave or during more advanced maneuvers like the roll. But if you are paddling in warm weather and calm water neoprene skirts can be too hot. A nice compromise is a sprayskirt with a neoprene deck but a nylon trunk.

Pump and paddlefloat: This is the nuts and bolts equipment used for basic rescues. "Don't leave home without them!" Some kayaks come equipped with a hand lever pump built into the deck of the boat to bail out water. If this is the case it's still a good idea to have another hand pump stowed under your deck rigging. At the very least this can be used to assist another kayaker in pumping out their boat. Paddlefloats come in a variety of materials and sizes. Eventually, when you buy one don't think cheap. For most kayakers the paddlefloat is absolutely essential for achieving a self-rescue and when you need it you really need it. Make sure your float has a good valve, plenty of volume and that it is ruggedly constructed. A double chamber paddlefloat valve has a distinct advantage. If one chamber springs a leak you still have another chamber to blow up.

Basic Clothing To Kayak In

PFD: Personal flotation device is the new term for life jacket. Make sure and wear one.

Synthetic Tops: Wearing 100% cotton is the quickest way to staying wet and getting cold. Cotton does not dry quickly or retain some warmth like synthetics when wet. Of course, if you're paddling in Baja in 86 degree weather it's a good way to go. Polypropylene or capilene shirts for cooler climates are better and they also wick away dampness from your skin. They are both made from a type of nylon but capilene is more expensive and doesn't hold odor as much as polypro does. And thank god for that!

Synthetic Bottoms: Quick dry shorts or pants work great for warmer days.

Wetsuits: The fact is, on a warm sunny day, when going for a casual paddle with no intention of practicing rescues most people don't wear them because it gets too hot. However, there's no argument against the conservative advice that one should always dress for immersion. What happens if I do flip over without one on? What's the water temperature? What's the air temperature? Wind factor? Most paddlers choose Farmer John style wetsuits as they give range of motion for the arms. Typically Farmer John's are 2-3mm in thickness.

Warm day attire for sit-inside with farmer john wetsuit shorty, sprayskirt, and pfd.

Dressed for immersion for a sit-on-top with wetsuit and pfd.

Paddling Jackets: This is a coated nylon water/windproof outer shell. Good paddling jackets have a method to cinch up around the wrists, neck, and waist to minimize the intrusion of water. A long sleeve paddling jacket is great for practicing rescues because combined with a wetsuit it will help keep you relatively warm. However, except for during colder days, a long sleeve paddling jacket often proves too hot if you're paddling at a working pace over distance. Eventually, you might also purchase a short sleeved paddling jacket for moderate weather touring.

Sun Protection: Since you probably just drove your SUV to go kayaking you've just contributed to the thinning of the ozone layer. So don't forget your hat, sunscreen and sunglasses. Baseball caps are not very adequate sun protection because they leave the neck, ears, and much of the face unprotected. Invest in a broad brimmed hat that will stand up to wind which also has a good retention strap with a barrel lock (they don't slip).

Optional Clothing For Those Comfort Oriented

There's a few creature comforts you might want to pick up. Booties or water shoes for your feet. They're a lot more comfortable than old sneakers. Paddling gloves with three quarter fingers and a reinforced thumb (wear point). Paddlers tend to get blisters on the inside of their thumbs from the friction caused by the paddle shaft. Paddling gloves also provide some hand warmth and protection against the sun for the back of the hands. And finally, one of my favorite items. Instead of wearing a bulky bathing suit under your wetsuit why not get a pair of synthetic underwear. What luxury!

OUTFITTING YOUR KAYAK

Once you've changed into your fashionable kayaking attire and gathered all your basic kayaking equipment its time to check out and set-up your kayak. The checklist below might look intimidating but after you follow it a few times this process should only take a few minutes. Regardless of which type of kayak you paddle or whether you are renting, taking a class, borrowing a boat or using your own you'll run down the following checklist.

Hatchcovers: If your kayak has gear hatches make sure they are secured and if they have a neoprene undercovers these should be properly sealed.

Water Bottle: Secure this under deck rigging within easy reach. Keep in mind that a water bottle that is not secured with a clip like a carabiner is the first thing to get washed off your boat in choppy water or during rescue practice.

Rudder Check: If your kayak has one take a quick look to make sure it is in working order. Sometimes you'll find that the steel cables that turn the rudder via your footpegs are crossed over and caught in the rudder mount or the rudder line where it attaches to the rudder has "jumped" out of its housing. A definite irritant in either case if you're on the water already and then find out you have a problem. Also, make sure you are familiar with how to deploy your rudder. Most kayaks use a looped line system where you pull forward on one line to drop your rudder and forward on the other to lift it.

Seatback: Just like in the airlines for take-off, put your seatback in an upright position (for proper support). Many sit-on-top seatpad and seat back systems have an array of straps equaling an old time girdle. You'll just have to get down and fiddle around.

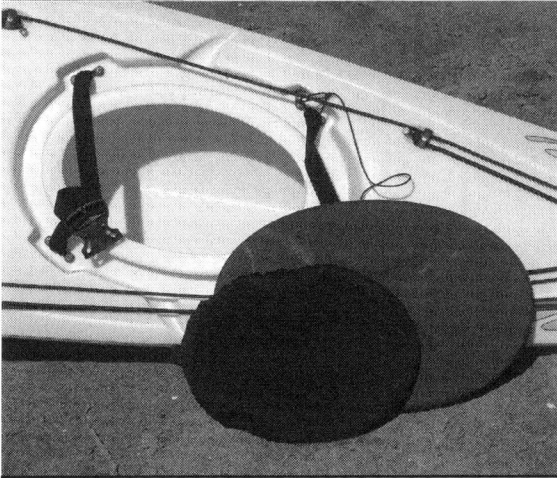

Secure hatch covers before paddling off.

Footpeg/footwell

adjustments: What is the proper leg length? Whether or not you have a rudder system you want some bend in your knees. Since use of your legs gives you more power in your stroke, some bend in the knee area gives you more push power than if they are straight out. Adjust your footpegs appropriately or figure out where to place your feet in the footwells.

Thigh bracing straps: If your sit-on-top kayak comes with these slip them over your legs. Tighten them to make sure they are snug.

14

Considerations for sit-inside kayaks

Bulkheads: Check inside. If your kayak comes with bulkheads make sure these are properly sealed. If no bulkheads maybe you should have flotation bags?

Stow Pump & Paddlefloat:
Before you do this, partially blow up your float and make sure there are no leaks. Also, dip your pump in the water to ensure it works. The best place to store the paddlefloat is in front of the cockpit under the deck rigging. Stow your float with the "fold method" as follows; with the nozzle side against the deck, slide the end closest to the nozzle under the bungee cord up to the midway point. Do this starting from the bow side of the deck rigging. Now fold over (on top) the second half, wrapping it around the bungee cord and then tucking this end of the paddlefloat under another section of bungee. The idea is that if a wave crashes across your deck the float won't wash off because of the way it is secured. You can now run your pump under the deck rigging either on top of your float or to the side. Stow your pump so that the handle (sometimes this can slide out) is facing the bow. As you set-up your pump and paddlefloat make sure neither will obstruct access to your sprayskirt's grab loop when the skirt is attached.

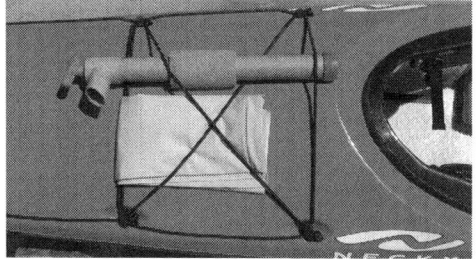

Footpegs and bracing: It's time to get in your kayak and check out the fit. When you get in a kayak which is on solid ground it's bad boat karma to step on the inside of the hull (bottom). Straddle the cockpit and slide your legs in. Once you've slid inside your kayak you are looking to establish a number of contact points which will give you better "boat control." Of course, one contact point is your backrest. Next adjust your footpegs. There's a lot of different footpeg and rudder designs depending on the boat make, so before you actually get in your kayak you should probably familiarize yourself with these features.

If you don't have a rudder system or you have a skeg system you'll still need to adjust the footpegs. Basically the footpegs should be adjusted so you can easily maintain solid contact with the footpegs and the thigh bracing area of the underdeck at the same time. This gives you better "boat control" for edging, bracing and more which we'll discuss later.

When your footpegs are adjusted properly the balls of your feet rest on the pegs and your feet are slightly advanced. In other words, you shouldn't be reaching for the footpegs with your toes nor should your feet be angled backwards thus cramping or pulling on your calves. Again, if your footpegs are adjusted correctly you will be able to easily lock into the thigh bracing on each side of the interior of your kayak while maintaining solid contact with the footpegs.

You also need to make sure that you have range of motion if you have a rudder. If your fit is too tight it usually restricts turning ability via your footpegs. A good way to check out rudder range of motion is to pull the rudder just out of the rudder mount via the rudder lines and then push one foot forward and then the other. Twist around to watch your rudder while you do this (a sure test of flexibility). You'll answer the questions of whether or not you've got range of motion and is it time to start taking yoga classes now.

Fitting the Sprayskirt: Always check out a new sprayskirt before paddling off! The easiest way to put on a sprayskirt (around the cockpit coaming), while sitting in your kayak, is to reach behind your back with both hands close to "center rear." If your skirt has an adjustable bungee cord make sure and leave the "tail" sticking out as you work the skirt under the rear coaming. Now work your hands around their respective sides of the back of the coaming until they reach the rear end corners. Now pull the skirt forward so you take in the slack and it catches under the rear coaming lip. Next take the skirt by the grab loop and wrap it over the front center part of the coaming and then along both sides. So back, front then sides.

Once your skirt is secured around the coaming it's time to check out the fit. Lean forward and then side to side. Does the skirt pop off the coaming? If your skirt

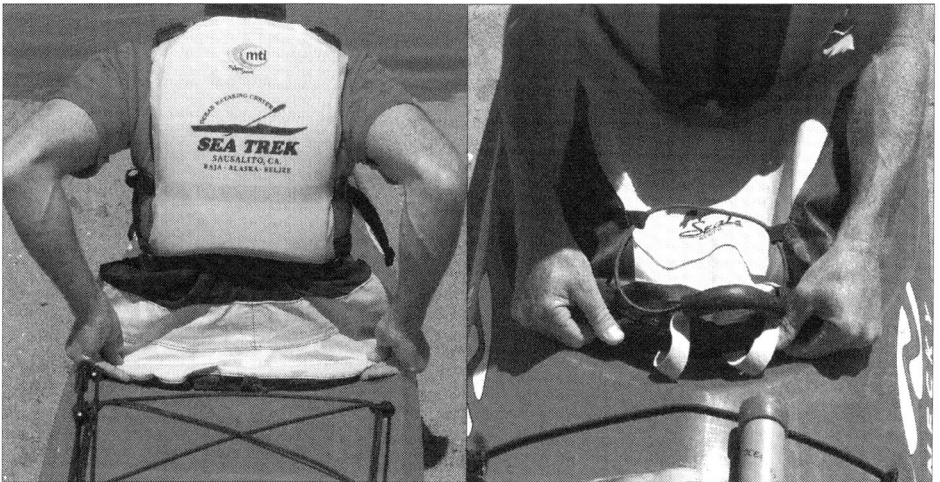

has suspenders they might be too tight. Loosen them. If you push your hand gently down on the deck of the skirt and it pulls off the coaming you might need to tighten the skirt itself via the bungee cord. If you struggled to get the skirt on in the first place it needs to be loosened a bit. You want a snug fit but you need to be able to get your skirt on and off with relative ease. Nonetheless, trying to secure your sprayskirt around the cockpit coaming will probably be one of the more frustrating things you have to do so it pays to practice.

Just as you check your sprayskirt fit you need to practice taking the skirt off in preparation for in water rescue practice. Close your eyes, run your hands along the sides of the coaming until they reach the grab loop. Pull forward, up and then finally backwards. If you are able to do this easy enough you're on your way. If not repeat the drill. Still having problems? Maybe the sprayskirt is not the right fit for the kayak you're in.

EXTRA POINTS

Boat control and the hip snap: Since you are already sitting in your kayak you might as well start understanding this "concept" of boat control. We already talked about the importance of correct adjustments of the footpegs and good contact with the thigh bracing area (not really relevant if you have a very basic recreational type kayak with a huge open cockpit). With a good fit you can execute a "good" hip snap which in turns gives you more boat control. Good boat control allows you to execute a variety of kayaking skills with greater proficiency. The boat control concept also applies to sit-on-tops with thigh bracing. In this case the thigh straps replace the interior thigh bracing of sit-insides.

What is a hip snap, also called a hip flick or knee lift? The hip snap is a way to manipulate your kayak by leaning it one way or the other underneath you. An effective hip snap makes it easier to edge a kayak, and is an integral part of bracing and other skills like the roll.

How to do it? Let's say you want to lean or edge your kayak on it's right side. This requires a hip snap where you lift your left knee/thigh into the kayak's bracing area. To facilitate this also pull upwards from the left hip and press the opposite butt cheek into your seat. Keep in mind your torso remains centered over your kayak and shouldn't tilt side to side. Do the opposite to edge your kayak onto its left side.

So now your kayak is "edging" on the right side. If you combine this with a sweep stroke on the same side you can carve a quicker turn to the left than if you

17

are not combining edging with a sweep stroke.

What about bracing and the hip snap? If a boat wake tips your kayak over to the right side you can brace to keep yourself from flipping. In this example, as you slap your paddle against the water on the right side, you'd lift your right knee/thigh and hip snap your kayak back to an upright position. We'll discuss edging and bracing further in the paddle strokes chapter.

You can start understanding the hip snap concept by sitting in your kayak on soft ground. Practice your hip snap and rock the boat side to side. Of course, it's a lot easier in the water but this exercise will initiate you into the world of boat control via the hip snap.

Chapter 2: Paddle Strokes

Just as an artist has a brush the kayaker has a paddle and instead of canvas you have the water. Ok, so I'm a romantic but kayaking is a romantic sport. There's an astonishing array of paddling strokes one could learn but we'll look at the fundamental strokes needed to get you started in controlling the direction and movement of your kayak. Just as you geared up and checked out your kayak on land it pays to practice your strokes before hitting the water while sitting in your boat.

Before we get started on paddle strokes let's take a quick look at paddle types, length, terminology, hand position and the "control" hand.

PADDLE TYPES

Feathered paddles: The purpose of a feathered paddle, where the blades are offset, is to allow one side to cut through the wind as the other pulls through the water. Less resistance. The degree of feather is lessening over time. A 90-degree

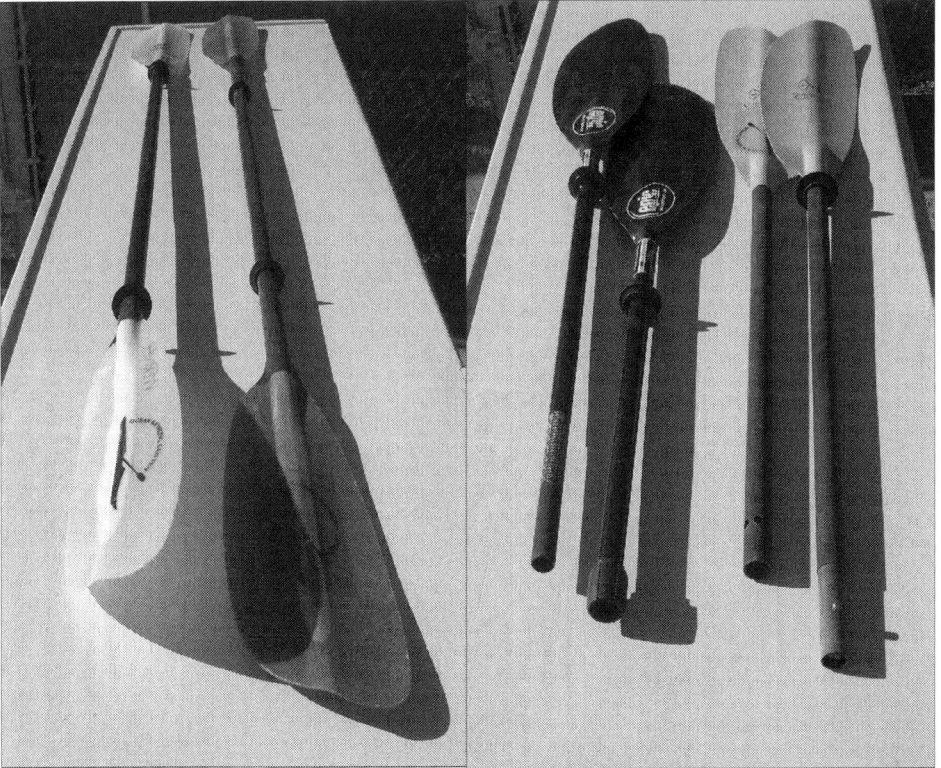

| 1. Feathered paddle to left with blades offset, unfeathered paddle to the right. | 2. Break-apart: The left one can be adjusted for length and degree of feather. |

feather used to be typical but requires more wrist action to work. Nowadays, the degree of offset tends to be between 45-80 degrees.

Unfeathered paddles: The blades are set in the same direction and are especially good for anyone prone to tendonitis or carpal tunnel syndrome. In short, they are easier to use because you don't have to manipulate the control hand (discussed later) to direct the paddle blade angle.

Break-apart paddles: These paddles offer a lot of versatility. They're great for traveling because you can take them apart. They also have pre-drilled settings so you can quickly set-up the paddle to accommodate a left or right hand person or use it as an unfeathered paddle. Break-aparts tend to be a little heavier, and because the shaft is not one solid piece there's some loss of "efficiency."

Adjustable break-apart paddles: These paddles have a number of benefits except the higher price tag. The adjustable collar allows for incremental changes in terms of feathering angle and the length of the paddle. Therefore this type of paddle is very versatile. It's easy to transport, can also be used as a spare paddle, can be adjusted to feathered or unfeathered, and various lengths for narrower single or wider double kayaks.

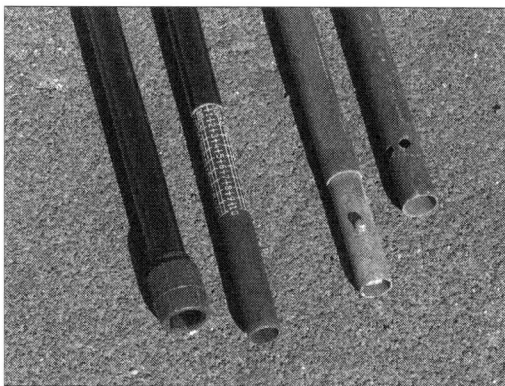

Adjustable break-apart to the left and pre-drilled single length setting to the right.

PADDLE LENGTH

The most frequently asked question and perhaps the hardest one to answer is "what's the right length?" There is no secret formula to address this most philosophical of questions, that works every time. Ultimately, the proper length has to do with a large set of variables: width of kayak, height of seat, length of torso, length of arms and proper technique. Given a certain kayak, and a paddler that has a good forward stroke, the paddle blade and only the paddle blade should be immersed throughout the stroke in calm water. If you are consistently burying part of the shaft with each stroke, the paddle is probably too long. If you are having a hard time completely immersing the full blade it might be too short.

Until you gain more experience with all the variables, a general way to check paddle length for use in a single kayak is as follows: Stand the paddle on end, reach your arm up and if you can hook your fingers (mid-joints) over the top you've got yourself a paddle. If you can hook your whole hand over the top at the wrist it's too short, if your fingertips don't quite reach the top edge--too long. In the case of a double kayak, the starting point is a paddle that extends just beyond your fingertips. Basically, at this stage of the game you should try different paddle lengths. You'll find, after making comparisons that a paddle that is too long is not only harder to pull through the water but also stresses your arm joints more. Personally, I tend to err towards a shorter paddle which translates to a higher cadence stroke and less stress on the body. This seems to be the way the market is going. Paddlers in singles that are 26" wide and less are using 215-220 cm length paddles. Those in wider boats and doubles tend to use a 230 cm length paddle.

21

Paddles also come with different blade sizes although most recreational type paddles have a medium blade size. Large blade sizes are for the big strong paddlers and this is what the Olympic flatwater sprinters use. They give a lot of power but they take a lot of power. For most of us a medium sized blade is perfect but for smaller built paddlers or those with upper body injuries a small blade is a good choice.

PADDLE TERMINOLOGY

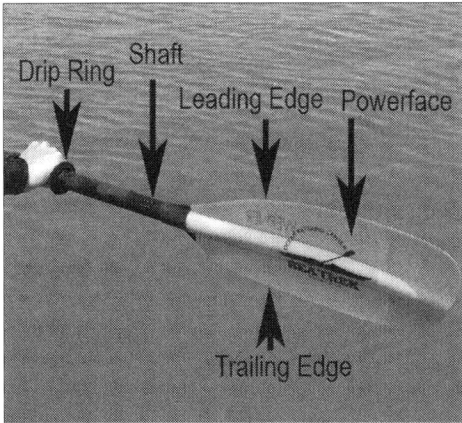

The scooped side of the blade is called the powerface and the reverse side is the backface or backside. The top edge of the powerface is the leading edge and the lower is the trailing edge. The shaft is what connects the two blades and usually you'll find two rubber drip rings around the shaft. These rings simply deflect water from the paddle blades from running down the shaft.

FEATHERED PADDLES: HAND POSITION & CONTROL HAND

Before you establish your hand position on the paddle shaft make sure that your paddle is oriented correctly. Stand with your paddle in your hands in a parallel position to the ground. Now rotate the paddle blades around until you're looking at the powerface or "scooped" side of the blade. Usually, when you look at a paddle blade you'll find that it is asymmetrical. This is because different parts of the blade make contact with the water at different times. This design feature is an attempt to make the blade track better (reduce flutter) through the water. Now make sure as you view the powerface that the longer tip of the blade is skyward and your paddle will be oriented correctly.

Now rest the paddle shaft on top of your head with hands spread out wider than your shoulders. The correct grip is when you have an 80-90 degree angle between your forearms and biceps. At this point move your drip rings so they touch the outside of your hands. The drip rings will serve as a marker where to keep your hands positioned. Eventually, you will no longer have to use the drip rings as

22

a marker and you can return them to the ends of the paddle shaft.

When using a feathered paddle one hand becomes the control hand that changes the directions of the paddle blades. If you are using a right hand control paddle your right hand is considered the "controlling hand." Thank god someone's in charge. Here we'll assume you have a right hand controlled paddle. For lefties just reverse everything.

Go ahead and set up your control hand by grasping the paddle shaft at the proper width location with both hands. If you hold the paddle in front of you, align up your right knuckles with the leading edge (top) of the powerface (right blade). Another way to look at this is that your wrist should be unbent (neutral position) and that same side forearm is in a perpendicular relationship with the powerface (right blade). With these points in mind your right blade is now correctly oriented to pull through the water on the right side. Now let's say you are about to dip the left blade into the water. Using your control hand, rotate your knuckles up and backwards, so your wrist is bent, causing the left blade to turn so the left powerface rotates perpendicular to the surface of the water. Note the following: Only your control hand directs. The paddle shaft should slide freely in your left hand and your left wrist remains in a neutral position. When your right control hand rotates the left paddle blade enough your left

Line up your knuckles with the leading edge of the powerface. Note forearm is perpendicular to the plane of the power-face

forearm will now be in a perpendicular relationship to the powerface (left blade).

Trust me, it's a lot easier to do all the above correctly with paddle in hand than to

23

write about it. When you go back to the right side, simply return your wrist to neutral position by dropping your hand down a bit and you're ready to take a stroke on the right side.

UNFEATHERED PADDLES: HAND POSITION

Hold your paddle in front of you so you are looking at the powerfaces (left/right) with the longer tip of the blades skyward. Find the correct hand width position (same as for a feathered paddle). The big difference in having an unfeathered paddle is that there is no dominant control hand. There is no need to rotate the paddle blade to pull it through the water correctly. Both of your hands should be oriented relative to the powerfaces of the left and right blade with your knuckles lined up with the leading (top) edge of the powerfaces. Another way to look at this is as follows: while holding the paddle extended in front of you, your forearms should form right angles to the left/right powerfaces of the blades.

THE FORWARD STROKE

Ah, the elusive forward stroke. This is the stroke that kayakers use the most and understand the least. The majority of paddlers on the water, technically, have a poor stroke and yet they do just fine. But why not be more efficient, have more power when you need it and look good! You know you've arrived at a place of elevated status when you're told, "hey, you've got a great stroke!" Or when you overhear, "look at that kayaker's stroke it's awesome." This is truly the highest praise a kayaker can receive and therefore refining your forward stroke deserves much attention.

A little bit of theory. For an efficient forward stroke the main emphasis is to utilize good torso rotation assisted by the pushing of the appropriate leg. This combination is used for most of the strokes (forward, sweep, reverse). Torso rotation takes advantage of the powerful muscles groups of the torso. Think of the spine as an axis point around which the torso rotates. Another way to look at this is as if your spinal column is a metal rod that continues down into your kayak seat. Your torso swivels around this rod. One side of the torso pushing forward and the other pulling backwards. Being a car society, an analogy that people easily grasp is that the torso is the engine, the arms the transmission and the paddle blades are the wheels. We want to transfer power from our major muscle groups (of the torso) to the wheels via the arms.

With all this emphasis on the torso being the driving factor behind your strokes I

24

do want to say that the idea is not to severely twist your upper body for each stroke. This is a good way to load up too much pressure on your lower back and irritate it. Leave that to the Olympians! The few that win the gold might get paid enough to afford physical therapy. What we are talking about is a little more subtle. And what it takes to have an efficient forward stroke is patience and as the years pass you will continue to refine this stroke as well as your patience. Fortunately, the basics are approachable.

The forward stroke can be broken into four components: Catch, Push/Pull Through, Exit and Recovery.

The Forward Stroke-Outline Description

1) The Catch. Rotate torso (right side forward, left backward), extend right arm and plant the whole blade into the water at the "catch" position next to your kayak by your foot.

2) Push/Pull through phase. Once the blade is fully immersed on the right side, immediately drop your right knee pushing your foot against the foot peg. This will give you leverage for a more powerful rotation than not using your legs. At the same time
rotate the right side of your torso backwards while the left side rotates forward. In this manner the right side of your torso and arm is pulling the right side of the paddle backwards while the left side is pushing the left side forwards.

3) The Exit. Exit the paddle by the time your right hand reaches your hip. Slice vertically out of the water, lifting with the elbow and shoulder.

4) Recovery. Set-up to take a stroke on the left side by continuing to rotate your torso in the same direction after your paddle exits the water. At the same time extend the left arm forward to plant the blade at the catch position. And follow the above steps.

The Forward Stroke-Detailed Description

1)The Catch. Starting off on the right hand side. Rotate your torso so the right side is advanced and the left side is back. As the torso is rotated, the right arm

1. *Catch: Spear the full blade in close to your foot and the kayak.*

2. *Push/Pull Phase: Let your legs and torso rotation do the work.*

3. *Exit: Go for a clean vertical exit when pulling hand is adjacent to your waist.*

4. *Recovery: At exit continue rotation to "hit" the catch on the next side.*

reaches to full extension. Spear the blade fully into the water, close to the side of the kayak with the emphasis on the upper hand spearing the blade in.

Initiating the catch position you have just wound up your torso like a spring and the full blade (no more no less) for the entire stroke is immersed in the water. Let's look at this again. Your right arm is extended, the right side of your torso is rotated forward, and the right paddle blade is spearing into the water almost touching the kayak (just in front of your foot). What is your left hand and arm doing? Your left hand is at a level somewhere between eye and shoulder level. (For a relaxed touring

26

stroke drop this hand down to shoulder level or below. For a more efficient, powerful stroke raise it up closer to eye level.) Your left hand also should not be too close to your chest. Try and maintain close to a ninety-degree angle between your forearm and bicep on the left arm and this will keep your hand away from your torso and translate into more immediate power when you start the pushing phase (left side of torso pushing forward). And yet one more thing to do. Keep that left elbow up just below the level of your hand and shoulder. Don't let it drop directly below your hand position.

2) Push/Pull Through Phase. Once the blade is fully immersed on the right side, immediately drop your right knee pushing your foot against the foot peg. Now the right side of the torso pulls the paddle backwards via the "linkage" of the right arm as the left side of the torso is pushing (via arm) the paddle around towards the kayaks centerline. Maintain a consistent level with your pushing hand (along a plane parallel to the water). Another look at the pushing side: Your pushing arm (and hand) arcs around towards the centerline directed by your torso rotation. The pushing arm should not end up being fully extended as it carves through its arc in the air. Maintain some bend in your elbow. As your pushing arm wrist crosses directly in front of you, you should be able to "read your wrist watch."

The pulling arm starts off fully extended and only starts bending at the elbow just as it prepares to exit at the hip. If you start bending your elbow too soon, you are trying to pull the blade too close to the kayak and you will tire out the small muscles of the arm. As your paddle exits the water do not bend the elbow much more than 90 degrees. Remember, as you exit you are going into the recovery stage and setting yourself up for the catch on the opposite side which means the pulling arm/hand will soon become the pushing arm/hand and you want that hand kept away from your shoulder/chest for immediate maximum pushing power.

3) The Exit. Ideally begins at the knee and the blade should be fully exited by the time your hand reaches your hip. The exit of the blade should be initiated from the lifting of the shoulder and elbow not the hand. This helps you get a nice clean slicing or vertical exit and also helps to bring your elbow up as discussed earlier in preparation for the pushing phase. Remember, if your elbow is directly below your hand and close to your chest you have a lot less pushing power. Try this. Stand right up against a wall facing it with the palm of your right hand at shoulder level and your elbow directly below (vertically aligned) and also against the wall. Now rotate the right side of your torso forward starting at the hips. Did your hand have any pushing power against the wall? Now stand back from the wall about a foot

and lift your elbow up to the side until you have 90 degrees between your forearm and bicep. Now rotate your torso pushing through your arm into the palm against the wall. You should feel a noticeable difference as more power is transferred in the second example. This philosophy applies to paddling.

4) The Recovery. This begins after the Exit. Think of the recovery as preparing for the next stroke in the water, and that you are winding up your torso and positioning the paddle for the "catch" on the left side now.

As your blade exits continue rotating your torso in the same direction as you extend your left arm forward towards the bow. Now you are ready to move into the Catch phase on the left side. All you have to do is repeat these steps 2,750 times and you'll have traveled three miles.

Common Problems:

1) Not enough torso rotation, too much arm paddling. This is indicated by the small muscle groups of your arms getting tired too easily and excessive bending of the elbows. Keep your hands out in front of you and at no point should the hand associated with the paddle as it exits the water come closer than 10-12 inches from the nearest shoulder. Some people like to imagine they are holding a big rubber ball or box between their arms to lessen arm bending and utilize the torso more efficiently.

2) Late entry. This is a common problem where your blade is already traveling backwards in the air before you finally get it fully immersed. Rotate forward (your torso) more on the side you are planting the blade in the water. In conjunction with the rotation, fully extend your arm just short of locking out your elbow. Focus on spearing the blade in the water immediately at the catch next to the side of your kayak. Practice spearing the blade, in the correct position, before pulling back.

3) Late exit. The tendency is to continue pulling the paddle through the water well past the hips. Exit by the time your hand reaches your hips. The most efficient part of the stroke is right at and after the catch, not when your paddle is drawing close to your hips. As you pull further back you lose forward movement efficiency, the blade naturally twists and you start lifting water.

4) The paddle blade (powerface) loses its perpendicular (vertical) relationship

28

to the surface of the water as it's pulled through the water. This usually happens more on the left side (with a right hand control paddle). Student needs to adjust their control hand accordingly. Watch your blade from time to time. It should remain perpendicular to the surface for the entire stroke and not twist.

5) Lack of Power. Eat your wheaties, get those New Year's resolutions in order, work out more to develop upper body strength, get your paddle more vertical (pushing hand higher) as described earlier, and pump those legs to help put some juice to your torso rotation.

Practice Session:

Pick a calm day and a ruddered boat so you can focus on your forward stroke. Breakdown the stroke as described earlier into its different elements and practice one thing at a time. For example, practice spearing the blade in at the catch. Later practice exiting the blade, emphasizing elbow lift. Eventually you'll be able to bring all the different aspects of the forward stroke into one integrated smooth flowing motion.

(Note: The **Reverse Stroke** uses the same dynamics but with the backface of the blade. The exception is which footpeg you push against. Starting on the right side, rotate your torso (right side) backwards. Plant your blade in the water at the catch behind you, approximately 20-45 degrees from the kayak's centerline. (Note, there's a tendency to keep the hands lower for the reverse stroke than the forward stroke which creates a wider but more stable stroke.) With the blade planted at the catch you are ready to rotate forward. Power your rotation by pushing into the left footpeg and dropping the left knee as you twist at the waist. Finish your reverse stroke when your paddle is approximately 90 degrees from the centerline. The reverse stroke is definitely more clumsy looking than the forward stroke. But don't worry no one ever says, "hey that guy has an awesome reverse stroke.")

THE FORWARD SWEEP STROKE AND EDGING

This is a turning stroke to maneuver your kayak in the direction needed. The forward sweep stroke uses the powerface of the paddle blade. Insert paddle at catch position and sweep it outward, away from the boat and back in a semi-circle motion. Let the artist in you emerge. Basically, with your paddle blade fully immersed, draw a half circle. Use your legs and torso rotation to power the sweep stroke. The paddle is held at a lower angle than in the forward stroke. Therefore if

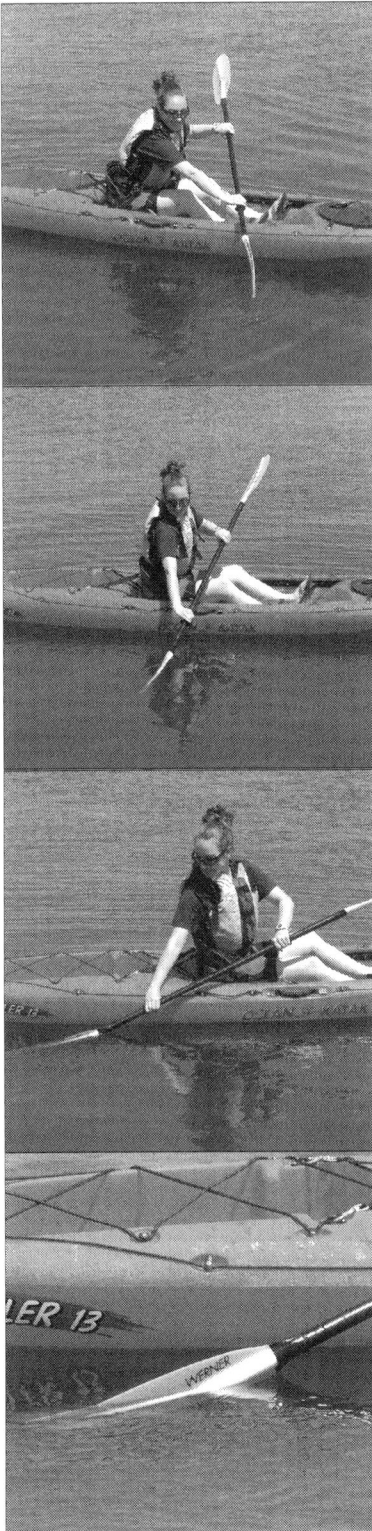

you are executing a sweep stroke on the right side your offside hand (left hand) should drop down from shoulder height to just above the deck height. Think of the paddle shaft as being in more of a parallel/horizontal relationship to the surface of the water. A full sweep ends with the sweeping blade all the way back, almost touching the rear side of the kayak to complete the half circle.

In conjunction with this try edging your kayak. Edging accelerates your turning power while sweeping. It's also a great way to watch beginners flip over. So practice with caution. Edging your kayak means leaning it over on its edge via the hip snap. (Again you can do this with a sit-inside with good thigh bracing or on a sit-on-top with thigh straps. No thigh straps on your sit-on-top? Time to cheat. Lean your body towards your sweeping paddle blade and you'll tilt your kayak a tad to facilitate the turn.)

The direction you edge the kayak seems counterintuitive for many but here's how it goes: To turn the bow to the left you execute a sweep stroke on the right side and hip snap (lift left knee/thigh) your kayak over on its right edge. Edging helps create "rocker" by laying the boat over on its curved side while drawing some of the bow and stern out of the water to lessen resistance. Edging in effect makes it easier to spin or turn your boat. When you get comfortable with edging you will be able to keep your kayak edged for however long you are sweep stroking.

Common Problems:

1) Not enough turning power even when

Use hip snap to edge your kayak towards your sweeping paddle. If edge of deck is catching water you're doing well.. Try and hold it for the entire stroke.

you think you're using good torso rotation. Paddlers tend to use the pulling side of their torso effectively but don't do well at transferring the pushing side through their arm to the paddle. Make sure to not bend the pushing elbow too much, as described in the forward stroke, and drive the pushing arm via your torso rotation. And of course, once again use your legs.

2) Paddlers tend to loose the perpendicular (vertical) angle of the paddle blade in relation to the surface of the water on the second half of the stroke. Let your eyes follow your blade through the entire stroke as your torso rotates and this will accomplish two things. First, you'll probably use better torso rotation and second you can monitor the position of your paddle blade as it travels through the water. Eventually this will not be necessary.

3) Still having a problem? Remember, lower that pushing hand for the entire stroke and this will enable you to reach (arc) the paddle out further from your kayak to provide more turning power. And get comfortable with better edging technique.

Practice session:

The first thing you should do is master your sweep stroke technique on both sides. Remember, keep your hands in front of you and keep the hand associated with the exiting paddle blade 10-12 inches out from your shoulder. Initially, just focus on sweeping the blade out and away from your kayak. Watch your paddle as it travels through the water to ensure you execute a full sweep stroke with good technique.

31

Now emphasize the pushing side because the pulling side comes naturally. And then its time to combine your sweep stroke with edging your kayak.

You need to have an effective hip snap for edging. Start off in a conservative manner so you don't flip and have to do a self-rescue. Do a partial sweep stroke, exiting at your hip and hold the boat over on edge during this stroke. Repeat this on both sides until you achieve a high comfort level. Next hold your kayak on edge while doing a full sweep stroke.

There's a couple things you can do while practicing edging with a full sweep stroke if you are at risk of tipping. At the end of the stroke immediately rotate the paddle so the backface is almost flat against the surface of the water and then glide the paddle along the surface until you get back to the catch position. You will feel some surface resistance and hence support while doing this. Another approach is to simply return your kayak to a level position during the paddles recovery stage. Then when you hit the catch start edging again. Eventually you'll be able to hold your kayak on edge during all phases of the sweep stroke.

(Note: The Reverse Sweep Stroke *uses the backface of the blade and follows the above technique but in reverse. The exception is similar to the reverse stroke. Once you place the backface of your paddle blade behind you at the catch and begin a low and wide sweep you push with the opposite foot to initiate your torso rotation.)*

THE SPIN MANEUVER

How to make a quick turn from a stationary position and in tight spots? Practice spinning your boat around in place by using your forward and reverse sweep strokes. See how tightly you can spin your kayak around. You'll do a forward sweep stroke on one side and a reverse sweep stroke on the other side. Remember, the reverse sweep uses the backface of the blade and starts out lined up at the back of the kayak. You sweep the paddle out and away from the kayak and end up right next to the front of the boat. When you are executing the reverse sweep stroke you can also edge your kayak for the greatest effect. In this case, just as in the forward sweep stroke, you edge your kayak over towards the sweeping blade. For example if you are reverse sweeping on your right side, hip snap in that direction by lifting your left knee/thigh. Sit-on-tops with no thigh bracing? Again use some body english to lean your kayak over a bit.

32

DRAW STROKES

The use of draw strokes is great for moving a kayak sideways to enable you, for example, to raft up to another kayaker or a dock. Here we'll discuss three different draw strokes.

1) The In/Out Draw Stroke. I also call this the "quick and dirty" draw stroke because most people can do it right away with a reasonable amount of success and still be sloppy. Extend your paddle out and away from the kayak at a right angle adjacent to your hips. At the same time twist your torso so that your chest is facing your paddle. Line the paddle blade powerface up so it is parallel to the centerline or side of your boat. Now immerse the full paddle blade (only the blade) and pull towards your kayak.

Actually, they say you should think in terms of pulling your boat towards the blade as if the blade is anchored in the water. To me it feels like I'm pulling the paddle. Exit your paddle blade out of the water before it makes contact with the side of your boat or you might find yourself "tripping" over it and getting a tad bit wet. Then repeat the above steps. Meanwhile, how are your hands positioned during all this? Firstly, they remain in their normal position spaced on the paddle shaft. Secondly, if you are looking for a powerful and efficient in/out draw stroke your hands will be close to a vertical relationship with each other and the water. Starting the stroke by rotating

1. *Slicing draw stroke: Rotate torso, extend lower arm at the catch and pull.*	2. *Powerface faces you as you slice the blade back out to the catch position.*

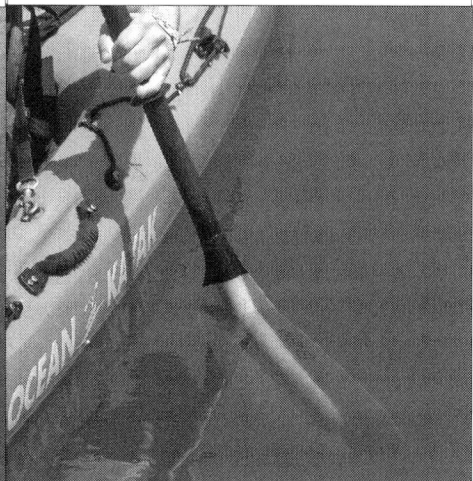

your torso towards the paddle helps maintain this vertical relationship. Therefore the paddle shaft will be vertical or perpendicular (more or less) to the surface of the water for the entire stroke. This gives you more bite on the water then if your outer hand (furthest from the water) pulls downward as you draw with your paddle. Keep that upper hand almost locked in place in front of your forehead.

2) The Slicing Draw Stroke. This is a classic and looks it when done properly. The start of this stroke is similar to the in/out draw stroke. Rotate your torso towards the paddle, plant the blade and initiate the draw stroke, but this time instead of exiting the paddle slice it back out to the initial catch position. This is done by rotating your control hand so the leading edge (top) of the powerface slices back through the water. Remember, for the entire stroke the paddle blade remains immersed. This is a beautiful and fluid stroke when done correctly without the jerkiness of the in/out draw stroke. In fact, you should look at the in/out draw stroke as a stepping stone to learning the slicing draw stroke.

3) The Sculling Draw Stroke. This is a great stroke for adding stability as you move your kayak sideways. Everything's basically the same as above except that you move your paddle in a figure eight motion after you enter at the catch during the draw stroke. This offers support because the paddle blade, using this motion, generates a bracing effect while also moving your kayak sideways. The sculling draw definitely requires some coordination for consistent figure eight patterns as the kayak travels towards the sculling blade. Lets look at this a little closer. In this stroke the paddle blade is staying immersed the entire time. Think of the blade as continually climbing back towards the catch position while at the same time you are pulling on it. This in effect moves you sideways.

There's no easy way to describe this stroke on paper. Ideally it will demonstrated to you by an instructor, friend or kayak video.

Common Problems:

1) Difficulty in maintaining a vertical draw stroke for more power. Focus on rotating your torso outwards towards the catch position and keep your upper hand over the edge of your kayak. The upper hand is also in a vertical position relative to your lower hand and you want to try and maintain this relationship for the entire stroke.

2) You feel tippy while practicing the various draw strokes. Edge your kayak away from the side you are practicing on. Another approach is to change the angle

of the paddle shaft relative to the surface of the water. The smaller the angle the more inherent support you'll get while practicing your draw strokes. This means dropping the upper hand and hence the paddle shaft downwards. As you get more comfortable with your timing and balance start working to maintain a consistent 80-90 degree (vertical) paddle shaft angle to the surface of the water for greater efficiency (power).

3) Problem controlling the direction of the blade as it flows through the water. If this is happening to you join the club. What I mean is that if you are pulling the paddle towards you it might flutter sideways or if you are slicing it back outward to the catch position you might have trouble controlling the paddle blade so that it slices straight out (perpendicular to the side of the kayak). These paddles just have a mind of their own. Take your time as you practice. Don't rush the stroke, go for technique at first over power and you'll figure out the nuances of these strokes. I use both my hands when controlling the direction of the blade during draw strokes.

4) Your kayak doesn't move sideways perfectly. Ah, the sea goddess is toying with you. Common problem number three could be the reason but it also is simply challenging in a dynamic water environment with wind, current and chop to move your kayak sideways perfectly. If you see the bow swinging around or the stern you can change the angle of your draw stroke to compensate. For example, if you are drawing on the right side and you find your bow swinging around to the right as you pull your paddle towards you angle it a bit towards the stern. This will swing the stern towards the paddle and hence counter the movement of the bow. Another approach is to change the catch position, moving the start point backwards or forwards (hence the paddle shaft is no longer perpendicular to the side of the kayak at your hip) depending on your needs.

Practice Session:

Find some calm water next to a dock and line yourself up parallel to the edge. Work through all the draw strokes described above starting off with the easiest one (In/Out). As in practicing the forward stroke try and focus on just one or two things at first as you draw away from the dock and then back again. Focus on keeping the blade fully immersed while it is in the water, focus on your outward torso rotation etc. Eventually, once you master the overall stroke you will now focus on moving the kayak sideways without the bow or stern swinging around.

Another thing to experiment with is changing the angle of the paddle shaft in relation to the water as discussed earlier. There are times in choppy water where you want to incorporate a bracing stroke along with a draw stroke. Drop your upper hand downwards to lessen the angle of your stroke as you pull your paddle towards your kayak. You should now feel more support from your paddle. Try this with all the different draw strokes. Remember, since learning draw strokes was not part of your childhood it'll take some time for muscle memory to set in and make these strokes more fluid.

1. *Low brace. Drive paddle backface down into the water as you hip snap.*

2. *Recovery: Rotate your blade and slice the leading edge out of the water.*

EXTRA POINTS

In all the draw strokes, once you become more comfortable with the outward rotation of your torso as part of the stroke you'll actually use your torso rotation, concentrating on the waist area to power your draw strokes. So if you are drawing the paddle blade towards the kayak on the right side you pull the blade towards the boat by twisting (emphasis in the waist region) the torso back towards a front facing position. Then you rotate your torso back outwards as you slice your paddle out to the catch position. This will take a little "feel" time to figure this out.

BRACING STROKES

Bracing is your second line of defense against flipping over. The first, of course, being exercising good judgment and not getting yourself into conditions above your abilities. But then again you'll never improve your skill and comfort level if you don't take some risks.

The Low Brace and Sit-Inside

For beginner to intermediate water conditions the tendency is to use the low brace to keep from capsizing. Imagine you're paddling along when a ferry cruises by and kicks up a succession of small waves. You didn't have time to punch through them and now you find yourself sideways to these oncoming waves, the least stable position to be in. All of a sudden you're flipping over towards your right side en route to a good head dunking but from your arsenal of tricks you pull out a low brace and avoid going over.

The low brace combines using the backface of the blade pushing down against the water along with a hip snap. First, let's talk about what to do with the paddle. The correct way to hold the paddle is perpendicular to the kayak's side and just in front of your hips. Rotate your hands downward until the backface of your right blade is facing the water. Consider that your bracing paddle blade (in this example the right one) is creating resistance against the water by pushing down into it thus allowing you to roll your boat back to a level position. Next slice it back to the surface by cutting forward and upwards with the leading edge of the blade.

Essentially, you are scooping the blade back up. There are some differences of opinion on the position of your elbows during the low brace. Should they be above your hands (as in vertically in relationship to the water) which might give you more downward pushing power or should the focus be on keeping them next to the sides of your torso. Both can work but I like to emphasize keeping the elbows close to your sides as this better protects the shoulder joints.

Now let's combine bracing with the paddle along with a good hip snap. Remember, as the backface of the paddle blade pushes flat down into the water you are creating resistance. And this resistance gives you a great platform off of which to execute a powerful hip snap. Timing is everything! Your boat is tipping to the right and the moment you start bracing on the right side initiate your hip snap (right knee/thigh) and bring the boat back to a level position. Once your boat is level stop bracing your paddle against the water. Recover your blade from sinking further by slicing it forward up and out of the water.

I can't focus on exercising caution enough. I've seen too many beginners, when accidentally flipping over, try to save themselves with a brace by overextending their arms and relying on the muscle power of their arms to keep upright. A quick route to a shoulder injury. Worst case scenario let yourself capsize rather than risk a rotator cuff injury or dislocating your shoulder.

The Low Brace: Sit-on-tops vs. Sit-insides

The main difference between using the low brace with a sit-on-top versus a sit-inside kayak depends on whether or not your sit-on-top comes with thigh bracing straps. If it doesn't which is the case with most sit-on-tops then you are just using the paddle as described above with the addition of a little body lean in the opposite direction to the side you are bracing on.

However, if you have thigh straps you'll execute a hip snap as described above along with bracing with your paddle.

1. *High brace: Keep the elbows tucked in and the paddle in front of your torso.*

2. *Drive paddle powerface down into the water as you hip snap.*

3. *To exit rotate blade vertically with the leading edge slicing out of the water.*

The High Brace

Now that I've made you terrified to practice bracing let's look at the high brace. This brace uses the powerface of the blade and the paddle is held with your hands at approximately shoulder level with elbows below and tucked towards the torso. The dynamics are the same as in the low brace in terms of creating downward resistance against the water. As in the low brace, if you have a sit-on-top with thigh brace straps or a sit-inside you'll be executing a hip snap as the powerface of your paddle slaps down against the water. For the recovery phase of the high brace rotate the blade vertically with the leading edge of the powerface slicing up and out

of the water

While the high brace can be a more powerful brace it also means there's more opportunities for shoulder injuries. The classic error is one where the paddler is executing a high brace, uses too much arm power, the brace side hand is above shoulder level and the paddle is no longer in front of you but reaching backwards. Ouch! This really opens the shoulder joint up

Low Brace Versus High Brace

When do you use one or the other? This is a good question. Generally there's a tendency to use the lower brace in less rough conditions. In big seas (which you're probably not planning on being in) and breaking waves the high brace comes into use more. Other factors come into play. If you are in the middle of a forward stroke on the right side and a boat wake tips you over towards your paddle you'd quickly change the angle of your paddle powerface to brace down on the water using a high brace to keep yourself from flipping in this case. Let's say you are just starting

The top photo is the low brace and the lower demonstrates the high brace.

a reverse sweep on the left side and a boat wake starts you tipping over to the left. Since the backface of your paddle is already pushing against the water as you execute your reverse sweep you'll simply angle it over more into low brace orientation and brace to prevent a capsize.

Common Problems:

1) You've heard that expression "timing is everything." That's the case with bracing with sit-inside kayaks and sit-on-tops with thigh brace straps. It takes some practice to execute a hip snap the moment you create downward resistance with your paddle blade on the water. Typically the hip snap is incorrectly delayed or non-existent.

2) A weak hip snap. You need to go back to square one and work on this. Practice the Bow Hip Snap drill (see chapter 5). If you are still having problems possibly you are too small or too big for the kayak you are in. Too small? Choose a smaller volume kayak or outfit the one you're in with hip and thigh padding so you have greater contact with the boat. Too big? Contact isn't the problem here you just can't move. Get a larger volume boat.

3) Diving paddle syndrome. This is quite common. You are so focused on not tipping over that as you brace into the water you don't keep the paddle blade flat against the water. Somehow your wrist twists the blade and it dives. Watch your blade and make any necessary adjustments. Get used to how it feels when it's flat to the surface and pushing down.

Practice Session for Sit-on-tops (without bracing straps)

This is pretty simply. Once again it's a good idea to practice one thing at a time until you have some mastery over that particular skill. Get in your kayak and paddle just offshore. Keep your body centered over your boat and hold your paddle just off the deck. Work on your low brace using only the paddle. Push the blade below the surface five inches or so and then recover the blade by scooping it forward, up and out. This should become a nice tight movement with a small range of motion.

Now you're ready to take things to the next step. Using some body English lean your kayak over to the right side then immediately brace down with your paddle on that side. As you create resistance in the water lean away from the bracing side. Once your boat is level recover your blade by slicing it forward, up and out of the water.

Practice Session for Sit-inside Kayaks and Sit-on-tops with Thigh brace Straps

Okay assume you're out on the water. Using "body english" tilt your kayak over to one side and then recover it to a level position with a low brace. Practice on both

40

sides and keep those elbows in.

Finally, you are ready to be challenged! Get someone to stand knee deep in the water, grab your bow and try and tip you. Recover with a low brace. When this is easy have them try this from the stern were you can't see what direction they're trying to flip you.

Let me touch briefly on practicing the high brace. You can do the same thing as mentioned above and practice getting in high brace position, bracing against the water and then the recovery. You can even rest your paddle against another kayaker's deck in high brace position, lean your boat over towards them and then brace back to an upright position. In this case their deck replaces the water. Concentrate on keeping your elbows in and emphasizing the hip snap rather than pushing with your arms. Lift your head last.

As you gain more experience, take more classes and develop your skills you'll probably get out into rougher conditions and it's then that you'll get some "real" bracing practice.

TANDEM KAYAKS AND PADDLING STROKES

A major difference in paddling a double over a single is that with a partner its important to sync up your strokes and to compromise in terms of speed and route. They don't call them divorce boats for no reason. Really, this is an opportunity to work on your communication skills, and for a more experienced paddler to share the beauty of kayaking with a lesser mortal.

The forward stroke: With two people powering a double you can really zip past those singles but make sure you are in/out together on the same side. This will help you take advantage of the boat's glide. Also, if you want to look good try and achieve the same vertical angle of your paddle shafts in relation to the water, and a similar stroke length.

The sweep stroke: Here's a secret. Even most kayak guides and instructors don't know how to teach a proper doubles sweep stroke. In a single for a full sweep stroke the paddler reaches forward and sweeps out low and wide bringing the blade all the way back. In a double the front paddler does the first half of this stroke, ending at their waist while the back paddler starts with their blade extended out from their hip and sweeps backwards. This is done at the same time of course. And don't forget to use your boat control/hip snap to edge your kayak for a quicker turn

41

| 1. Draw stroke: *Extending lower arm and spearing the blade in at the catch.* | 2. *Slicing blade out towards the catch in unison.* |

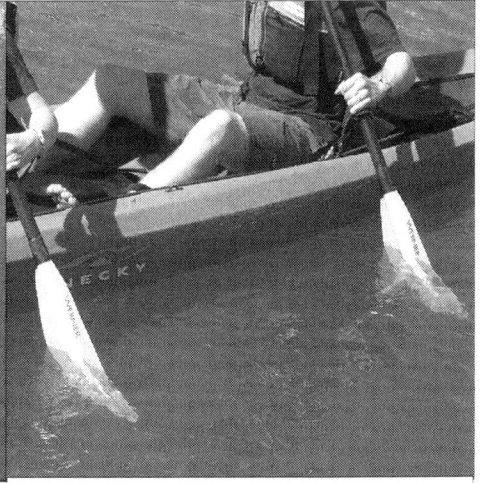

if you're in a sit-inside or have thigh bracing on a tandem sit-on-top.

Draw Strokes: This takes some coordination as again both paddlers should be drawing in unison with equal power.

Spin Maneuver: The front paddler will do a forward sweep on one side and the stern paddler will do a reverse sweep on the opposite side. This is the quickest way to turn your boat around from a standstill.

The spin maneuver on a double sit-on-top kayak. The front paddler executes a forward sweep while the rear paddler does a reverse sweep.

Bracing: Again like the draw strokes this takes some good coordination, especially if an aggressive brace is needed. You both have to execute a good synchronized hip snap while bracing with your paddles on the same side. If you're paddling a double sit-on-top with no thigh straps you'll primarily just be using your paddles to brace.

Spending time with your partner in a double in different conditions is the best way to get those strokes in sync. Eventually it becomes spontaneous because not only have you learned to read your partners reactions but they become the same as yours in any given situation.

EXTRA POINTS: COMBINING STROKES

Before we wrap up this chapter on paddling strokes I want to talk about combining strokes and what I call "variations on a theme." And I'd like to use a series of examples to illustrate my points. Let's say you're making a crossing from A to B and there's a stiff wind. Even with your rudder deployed (or if you don't have one poor fool) you find you need to execute numerous sweep strokes to keep your kayak on the right track. Instead of doing continuous sweep strokes when correcting you combine strokes. For example, you sweep (and edge) on the right side then execute a normal stroke on the left side. Sweep right, normal stroke on left. This combination provides more forward momentum to get you to your goal sooner and if you have a rudder provides faster turning power (more speed and the rudder turns the boat quicker). A variation on this theme might be to choke up on your paddle shaft placing your hands more to the left so you have more leverage for your sweep stroke on the right. Offsetting your hands like this on a very windy day and no rudder will help you keep your boat corrected with greater ease.

Here's another scenario. You've got a nice forward stroke going and you're moving right along when suddenly you're hit by some bumpy water that puts you off balance. It's not bad enough that you have to brace but still you need some reassurance that you're not going to flip over. Just change the angle of the blade with your control hand during your forward stroke so that the blade is at a 45 degree angle (angle depends on your needs) to the surface with the leading edge angled upwards so the blade doesn't dive. All of a sudden you've combined a partial bracing stroke into your forward stroke.

Your rudder cable is broken and you're executing countless sweep strokes in a good crosswind with no end in sight. Now conditions worsen and you feel vulnerable to tipping every time you do a full sweep stroke arcing from front to back. Change the angle of the blade as it sweeps (to 45 degrees) so your paddle creates some surface resistance and always maintains lift by angling the leading edge slightly upwards. Your sweep won't be as powerful of course but then again you won't have to perform a rescue.

So variations on a theme is really when you perform a stroke in a slightly different manner. We've talked about basic draw stroke position where the paddle shaft is vertical in relation to the surface of the water. This is a vulnerable position to be in if some force causes you to push down on your paddle. Vary your technique. Lower your upper hand so the paddle shaft is more diagonal relative to the water and you'll get some inherent bracing in your draw stroke.

There's a long list of combining strokes and variations of specific strokes that you can call upon. What's exciting is that after you discuss, practice and use some of these variations they will eventually become instinctual. And then maybe you'll hear "hey look at that instinctual paddler with the awesome stroke."

Chapter 3: Rescues for sit-on-top kayaks

One of the ultimate scenarios that a kayaker has to deal with when paddling is capsizing. It's not really a question of if it will happen but more a question of when. Call it the adventuring spirit that gets us into trouble sometimes or call it arrogance, either way you want to be prepared. Learning and practicing rescues is the keystone to safe kayaking and even if you don't flip your partner might. Knowing your rescues is the number one confidence builder for paddlers.

The sit-on-top self-rescue is simpler than the industry standard (paddle float) self rescue for sit inside kayaks. Primarily this is because you don't use the paddle float device (see sit inside rescue chapter) and sit-on-tops unlike sit insides don't fill up with water once capsized.

But the reality is that self-rescues in both types of kayaks do require a certain level of physical strength (upper body mostly), agility and coordination. Imagine you're in the water. Do you think you're strong enough to hoist yourself up onto your kayak? The old adage practice makes perfect applies especially to rescues to ensure you really master these lifesaving techniques!

Don't worry, if you don't have the physical abilities to master rescues it doesn't mean you can't paddle. It just means that you need to stick to very calm sheltered waterways and ideally paddle with an experienced boater. Guided tours with kayaking companies are also a great way to go. Most are oriented for beginners.

SINGLE SIT-ON-TOP SELF RESCUE

So you've just flipped and you find yourself in the water. Quickly grab hold of your kayak and paddle. You don't want to lose contact. Next, assuming your kayak completely flipped you'll have to turn it right side up. You'll need two hands so place your paddle parallel to your boat between you and the kayak so you can keep an eye on it.

Sit-on-tops can be challenging to flip back over. They tend to be wider than sit

From top left to right. 1. *Push/pull method to flip kayak.* 2. *Launch across the seat area.* 3. *Rotate butt into seat.* 4. *Swing legs into place.*

inside kayaks and have flatter hulls. You'll have to experiment with the boat you are using to find out the best approach. Position yourself near the seatwell with your torso facing the boat. One approach is for one hand to push upwards under the side closest to you while the other hand grabs onto something under the boat on the other side. This "something" could be the seatback strap, or a deck line for example. Here you'd be using the push/pull method to rotate the boat right side up. Scissor kick your legs at the same time to give yourself more leverage.

Another approach is to push upwards with both hands under the edge closest to you while kicking powerfully. You can also try going to the stern of the kayak and rotating the boat. Finally, there's the rope option.

For a rope assist you'd need to be carrying a six foot length of rope. Tie this to something on one side (underneath) near the mid-point. Throw the rope over the hull and get to the loose end side. Grab the end of the rope, place your feet against the edge of the kayak and lean backwards away from the boat while pulling on the rope. If this works the next thing you'll be doing is watching the boat land on top of you so get ready to ease the boat into the water with one hand.

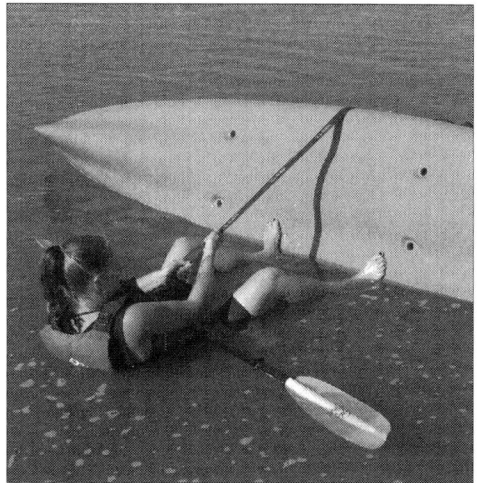

If this becomes your best option for righting your kayak in future outings your rope would be pre-tied and ready for use. Just don't get tangled up in it!

Okay finally you've flipped the boat right side up! Line up with your torso facing the seatwell area. Secure your paddle under any deck lines or bungee cord or simply hold it in one hand lined up perpendicular to the kayaks side. Now its time to launch up and across your seat area.

To launch up you can either stretch your legs to the surface behind you and kicking powerfully slide up and over the kayak or drop your legs vertically below you, scissor kick a few times and launch onboard. Like I said this is no easy task so you'll definitely want to practice. Part of the challenge is that you are a responsible

Sling rescue. 1. *Set up sling/insert foot.*
2. *Push down and launch onboard.*
3. *Rotate into seat.*

boater and hence wearing a pfd. That very same pfd will often snag against the edge of your kayak as you try launching on deck. Practice makes perfect!

Once you get enough of your body over your seatwell area turn your head towards the bow, and rotating your body in the same direction twist your butt into your seat. Now brings your legs into normal paddling position and you're ready to paddle again.

If you are having trouble lauching your body up onto your sit-on-top you can use leg power via a sling. You can buy or make your sling. Essentially you are going to create a stirrup so you can use leg power to help boost yourself up onto your kayak. A typical sling might be a 13-15 foot length of one inch wide webbing. Tie it off in a loop. To set your sling up while in the water loop it around one end of your paddle just below the paddle blade. Loop it through itself so you can snug it against the paddle shaft. Now position that end of the paddle across the other side in front of the seat area. The idea is to let the webbing flow under your kayak. Push the kayak towards the webbing to help it flow under the hull. Once you have it loop it over the shaft on your side. Now put your foot in the stirrup and leverage yourself onto your boat, chest across your seatwell area. From here you continue your rescue as normal except, of course, before you paddle off you'll have to undo your sling. Note that you can adjust the stirrup length by wrapping it around the paddle shaft on your side a few times to take in some slack.

SINGLE SIT-ON-TOP ASSISTED RESCUE

Imagine you are paddling with a friend whose also in a sit-on-top kayak and they flip over. You'll immediately paddle over encouraging them to hold onto their paddle and boat. Next their kayak needs to be flipped over. This can be done in the same manner as described in the solo rescue section or you can assist. To assist get to one end of their boat and help rotate it as they also start flipping over their kayak.

Now parallel park yourself alongside their boat and lean over and stabilize it. The rescuee will launch onto their boat as in the solo rescue, torso across the seatwell area rotating their butt into the seat. If they have a problem doing this you can reach over, grab their pfd by the shoulder strap and help pull them on board.

What if you have to rescue a double? Basically the procedure is similar however now you have two people in the water to watch out for. Position yourself at one end of their kayak helping to rotate it over. If both members of the double are on the same side of their kayak they will reach underneath and can either use the push/pull method or simply push upwards at the same time. If they are on opposite sides, one will push and the other will reach over the hull when then can to help pull the boat right side up. The most important thing is that you the rescuer need to show some confidence and management in directing the people in the water what to do. For example, you might have to make the decision to hold onto (i.e. secure) their paddles if your swimmers seem overly challenged already.

Once the boat is upright you'll parallel park against the double to stabilize it and get your boaters into their craft one at a time.

DOUBLE SIT-ON-TOP SELF RESCUE

In this example you've been paddling a double which just flipped. Immediately encourage your partner to grab hold of the kayak and their paddle. In many rescue scenarios there are a multitude of ways to do things. Let's say you are more experienced than your partner and they are having a hard time swimming to the kayak. If you are holding onto it and also have your paddle you can extend your paddle towards them and help pull them in. Another approach is to slide down one side of your kayak and feed the boat towards them so they can grab it. The point is that there are many different ways to help out in rescue scenarios.

Now that you are both connected with the kayak place your paddles where you can keep an eye on them. A good position is parallel to the kayak floating on the surface between each paddler and the kayak. Let's say you are both on the same side. You'll either be able to use the push/pull method or just the push method or a combination of the two. As you know it depends on the type of kayak you're dealing with. Other approaches include paddlers being on opposite sides which was discussed above. Finally, one paddler could be positioned on one end rotating the kayak while the other paddler is centered using the push/pull method.

Once the boat is upright it is best to get the least experienced or weaker person on board first. They might need some help. One approach to helping is to counter balance the kayak from the other side. Another approach, if you can, is to reach over and help pull your partner on board. Once on board it's your turn, getting up just like in the singles self rescue.

DOUBLE SIT-ON-TOP ASSISTED RESCUE

So you're in a double sit-on-top kayak and whether you need to rescue a single or double sit-on-top kayak someone's got to be in charge. The more experienced member of the tandem should take the lead. Encourage those in the water to hold onto their boat and paddles. Maneuver the double to one end of the kayak to help rotate it. Position the people in the water to assist you as described in the other rescue sections. Once the their boat is right side up, parallel park your double against their boat. Have the swimmers come around the side of their kayak away from you. In the process make sure they always hold onto their kayak. You don't want any current pulling them away!

Both you and your partner should now be leaning over to brace the rescuee/s kayak. If they are unfamiliar with a self-rescue you'll have to tell them how to launch up across their seatwell. Make sure they are in position to paddle, communicate a game plan and away you go. The best way to separate is to slip forward if your boats are bow to stern. That way if their boat has a rudder you can check and make sure it's in good working order. If both your kayaks are lined up in the same direction you might slip backwards to check their rudder before paddling off.

Finally in assisted rescue scenarios their might be situations where it is not wise for the rescuee/s to paddle off. Perhaps they have flipped repeatedly and will do so again. Maybe there is an injury. In these cases its best to keep bracing onto their kayak and try to flag help or make that distress call if you have VHF radio.

Chapter 4: Rescues For Sit-inside Kayaks

The primary kayak rescues that most outfitters teach, and require you to know before they'll rent out sit-inside kayaks are the paddlefloat rescue (self-rescue) and the T-rescue (used to rescue another paddler). We'll discuss these rescues in detail and relate the techniques used, to performing doubles rescues. Finally, to help you increase your repertoire of rescues I'll go over the ever popular "cowperson" rescue and others in the "extra points" section.

Let's start with the paddle float rescue. This is the most challenging one so I've taken a dual approach to describing it. Firstly, I go over this rescue in outline form so you can get the flow. Secondly, I'll describe this rescue in "put me to sleep" detail. Hopefully, you'll refer back to this section between naps, I mean practice sessions, and eventually you'll learn the nuances of this standard rescue.

As is the case with paddle strokes I recommend you practice as much of the paddlefloat rescue first on dry land as you can. This will help you choreograph all the various movements for an easier learning curve on the water

THE PADDLEFLOAT RESCUE

The basic concept of this self-rescue is that with your paddlefloat

53

placed and blown up on one end of your paddle you create an "outrigger" to help steady the kayak as you maneuver back into the cockpit.

The Paddle Float Rescue-Outline Description

1) Wet exit. Ugh! Dump over and maintain contact with your boat and paddle at all times.
2) Prepare paddle float. Blow it up on one end of the paddle.
3) Flip kayak right-side up. Check seat back, footpegs and rudder.
4) The set up. Line up one end of paddle behind the rear coaming of the cockpit. Secure it with one hand as the other end (with the paddlefloat) extends out perpendicular to your kayak.
5) Launch onto back deck. Get most of your weight on the kayak just rear of your paddle and cockpit. Place feet on extended paddle. Keep paddle perpendicular, extended and weighted at all times.
6) Getting in. Work the first leg in and then the second leg as you turn your head and torso towards the stern of the kayak. Before releasing the second leg off the paddle shaft secure it with the appropriate hand.
7) Corkscrew into a seated position. And switch hands securing the paddle.
8) Boat control. Thighs bracing, feet on pegs. Next move float in front of you, keep extended and weighted.
9) The clean up. Put skirt on, pull aside edge and pump out water. Secure skirt and pump. Release paddle float valve, deflate and quickly secure under deck rigging.

Paddle Float Rescue-Detailed Description

1) The wet exit. To practice the wet exit get in your kayak and paddle just offshore in water you can stand in (in case you have problems and need to drag your boat back to dry land). Take a deep breath, try and relax and yes tip yourself over with an aggressive hip snap and some body english. You are now entering the wet exit phase of the rescue, aptly named, although I have seen students in such a panic to get out of their kayaks that they don't even get their hair wet.

The easiest wet exit is a relaxed wet exit and that will take you a few attempts to achieve once you realize your heads only under water for about two seconds. Let your kayak turn completely upside down. Hold onto your paddle with one hand while running both hands along the sides of the coaming up towards the front or peak of

the coaming until you connect with the grab loop of your sprayskirt. The exercise of running your hands along the coaming will insure that you actually find the grab loop. Now pull the grab loop towards the bow, using one or two hands, then away from the deck and finally backwards. The next step is to run your thumbs along the inside of the coaming (assuring that they are under the loose sprayskirt) and backwards to a position adjacent to your hips.

At this point you're asking "what about the paddle?" You are still holding it in one hand, and ideally it is now positioned parallel to the kayak and is trapped under one of the hands that has a thumb hooked inside the coaming. Lean forward, relax your feet off the footpegs but keep your legs fairly straight rather than bunched up, and push off. Keeping the forward tuck, critical for a smooth wet exit, your butt will come out first with your legs to follow. It's almost as if you are somersaulting out of your kayak. Learn this jingle, "tuck and push."

2) Prepare paddlefloat. As you come out of your kayak and take that first refreshing gulp of air you should be maintaining a firm grip on your boat. Again try and relax, anxiety and panic will only prolong your time in the water. Your PFD and wetsuit will comfortably keep you afloat. At this point you have choices to make. Do I flip my kayak now or later? If it's relatively calm, with no risk of taking in more water into the cockpit, you can flip your kayak right side up. Probably the only reason to do so at this stage is that's it's easy to find your paddlefloat and pull it out. But let's assume there was a reason you flipped over. At this stage you don't want to get more water into the cockpit so leave it upside down. An overturned kayak also creates more drag forces in the water so if you happen to let go of it the wind or current won't pull it away as quickly. Finally it's easier to secure yourself to the kayak when it's overturned.

Move towards the front deck where you have your paddle float stored under the deck rigging and pull it out. At this point it's a good idea to have two free hands to continue the rescue. Run one arm through a deck bungee to the crook of your elbow. Now you have two free hands to work with and yet a secure connection to your boat. An option to this is to run a leg inside the cockpit to hold onto the boat. I prefer running my arm through the deck bungee because it's right there as I'm pulling the float out and I can keep my legs underneath me and kick with them for more control if necessary. Try both methods and pick what works for you.

Hold the paddlefloat with the hand of the arm that is secured to the deck bungy. Your paddle should be in your free hand. Let the paddle rest at surface level, positioned off your shoulder. Grasp the paddle near the blade, the rest of the paddle is extended backwards behind your back, and now slide it into the paddle float sleeve. Make sure and hold the float on securely as you blow it up. Blow the float up as much as possible because you'll need all the flotation you can get and this also prevents the float from slipping off.

Next remove your arm from the bungee and slide back to a position facing the center of the cockpit. Your kayak is still upside down at this point. The paddle can be placed between you and the kayak or held by your legs. This is an easy way to keep an eye on it and free up your hands.

3) Flip kayak right-side up. Now you are ready to flip your kayak right side up. One hand will gasp the near side cockpit coaming and the other reaches under and across to grasp the far side coaming. With a kick of your legs to assist, and the close hand pushing up and the other pulling (push/pull), you can quickly rotate your boat upright. Check a couple things. Make sure your seat back is in place and your footpegs haven't slid off their brackets. Quickly move back to the rudder and verify cables aren't crossed and the rudder line isn't foiled. Nothing worse than getting back in your boat in a stiff wind and finding your rudder can't be used.

4) The set up. Line up your paddle just behind the rear coaming and establish a hand grip with your hand centered on the coaming behind the seat. Your fingers should be wrapped around the inside of the coaming while your palm and thumb secure the shaft against the deck. Your paddle is positioned so that your hand is securing it to the kayak close to the exposed paddle blade and the majority of the paddle is extended off the kayak providing leverage and flotation with the attached paddlefloat. Make sure your body is positioned on the stern side of your paddle.

At all times, while conducting this self-rescue, try and avoid leaning or pushing against the edge of your kayak. This will only cause your cockpit to scoop up more water.

You're still in the water at this stage. Your free hand will be grasping the kayak on top of the deck (centered) and stern side of your body. Next drop the other forearm/elbow on top of the paddle shaft while maintaining your hand grip around the shaft and coaming.

5) Launch onto back deck. There are a couple ways to launch up onto the back deck which is the next step. One is to drop your legs vertically and scissor kick, bobbing up and down to build momentum. One, two, three and launch up with a final kick and pull your torso over onto the back deck adjacent to your paddle. Don't let go

of that hand grip. Another approach is to float your legs behind you to the surface, extend away from the kayak and try a seal landing by kicking and pulling yourself horizontally onto the back deck. Either way your PFD is guaranteed to get in your way by snagging on the edge of the boat. The solution is to practice and you'll get better at coordinating your movements.

As you launch up on the back deck, immediately hook the arch of the closest foot on top of the paddle shaft. And then hook your second foot (top side) on top of the paddle shaft just below your first foot. For the rest of your paddle float rescue there are three things you must do.

> Keep your paddle Perpendicular to the kayak at all times.
> Keep your paddle Extended off your kayak at all times.
> Keep your paddle Weighted at all times.

The acronym is PEW. And if you are having trouble remembering this one just sniff your armpits after a ten mile paddle in the same synthetic shirt you've been using for the last four outings without a wash in-between and think about who needs to be rescued now.

Every student needs to figure out and experience what works best in terms of body position once launched up on the back deck. A tall student will line up a little further away from the paddle and cockpit in order to get their legs in versus a short student who will get up on the back deck right next to the paddle shaft. As well, note that the majority of your body weight is actually supported by the kayak not the paddle float. The paddle float is simply a stabilizing force not a raft that will float or hold up all your weight.

6) **Getting in.** Maintain your handgrip around the paddle shaft and coaming. Your other hand is on the deck of the kayak around chest level. Now its time to start working your closest leg into the cockpit. At the same time start swinging your torso and head towards the stern of the kayak while reaching with your free hand under the thigh of your leg that remains on the paddle shaft. Once you a have a secure grip, with your palm on top of the paddle shaft, you can work your second leg into the cockpit, slide in and corkscrew (turning towards the float as you do this). Throughout these gymnastics maintain PEW. At this point for most people it is too uncomfortable to maintain their original hand grip around the paddle shaft and coaming. It is okay to release that grip as you start to work the second leg into the cockpit. Where does that hand go? Up by your chest on the back deck. And think in terms of using your stomach to trap and hold the paddle in place.

7) Corkscrew into a seated position. As you corkscrew into the boat there's a couple things to remember. One, make sure that you drive your legs forward instead of bunching them up (bigger folks get caught up against the thigh bracing if they do this), and try and drop your butt into the seat as soon as possible. The idea is to get your center of gravity lower quickly. Meanwhile, after you are almost completely turned around and in a seated position it is necessary to switch hands on the paddle shaft. For example, if you are performing the rescue from the right side of your kayak and both legs are inside the cockpit and you are corkscrewing into position you'll need to release your left hand from the paddle shaft but only after you secure it with your right hand. Your left hand will then get positioned on the left center side of the cockpit coaming. Remember, as you switch hands extend your right hand out on the paddle shaft to help you maintain PEW.

8) Boat control. The exercise is not over yet. It is critical to maintain control of your paddle float "outrigger". This is your support system. Now that you are back in a front facing seated position, immediately get your feet on your foot pegs and lock in your thighs. This establishes boat control and your ability to brace with your paddle float if conditions warrant. Meanwhile, your paddle is still positioned in its original position behind the rear coaming and fully extended. It helps in terms of control, to hook your elbow stern side of the paddle shaft in conjunction with maintaining your hand grip.

Once you've established boat control bring your paddle in front of you quickly. Use one hand to bring it over your head while keeping the float resting on the water. Let me explain this tricky maneuver. Assuming your paddle is extended off the right side of the kayak, leave your left hand where it is on the left center side coaming. Your right hand is currently palm side on top of the paddle shaft with your thumb facing the bow and your fingers facing the stern. Now release your grip and move this hand just in front of the paddle shaft and rotate it backwards so the thumb is wrapped over the top of the shaft and the forefinger is wrapped around the bottom. Go ahead and lift the paddle over your head, and as you move it in front of your chest you'll find your right hand is now in its normal paddling position. Voila! I feel like a physicist explaining the minutia of kayaking. Now that left hand that's been itching to do something can also hold the paddle but as before maintain PEW.

9) The clean up. Unless you're lucky you'll notice a lot of water inside your cockpit which will make paddling off very challenging. If it's calm you can pump the water out immediately. If not and there's water swamping your boat put on your sprayskirt and then pull the side off just enough to work in your pump. How do

you get the skirt on in rough water and at the same time use your paddle float for bracing and balance? Start working your sprayskirt on towards the back with one hand while the other controls your paddle float. At a certain point you'll usually need two hands to work the skirt on. Tuck the closest end of the paddle shaft under your PFD right into your gut. Lean slightly forward to help trap it and keep your thighs braced against the kayak while leaning the boat towards your paddle float. Work the skirt around the corners simultaneously and then snap on the front of the skirt followed by the sides. Now you can pull off the side of the skirt and pump. This is another example of were maintaining PEW can be challenging.

Now you are ready to pump. One approach (assume your paddle is extended off the right side), is to drop your right forearm on top of the paddle shaft. Grip the pump with your right hand and pump with the left hand. While your right forearm keeps weight on the paddle float your left elbow can also help keep the paddle tucked against your stomach and hence maintain the perpendicular relationship to your kayak. If it's choppy you can even edge your kayak over towards the paddle float which throws more weight via your forearm onto your paddle.

Wow just about done. Tuck away your pump. Seal off your skirt. Before you take off the paddle float make sure your paddle is oriented in the right direction. Then its time to take off the float and quickly secure it under the bungee.

If you can paddle to a calm area and assess your situation do so. This also gives you an opportunity to pump out any additional water and to fully secure your pump and float. And yes maybe just rest a bit.

Common Problems:

1) Not holding onto to the kayak and paddle at time of wet exit. Try it again.

2) Not maintaining PEW. Use your arms or legs, as appropriate, on the paddle to constantly maintain the paddle in a perpendicular relationship to the kayak, keep it extended, and of course keep weight on the float.

3) Not enough weight on the kayak, that is too much weight in the water and on the float. Your float alone will not support all your body weight. Pull more of your body up on the back deck of your kayak but always keep some weight on the

float. With a little bit of practice you'll figure out the correct ratio.

4) Turning the head to watch the first leg enter the cockpit instead of twisting it to face the rear. It's natural to try and watch your foot as you struggle to get it in the cockpit. But this can be counter-productive because it shifts more weight away from the float. Get used to "feeling" your way in as your head and torso (brush against the back deck) as you twist around to face your paddle float.

5) Lifting the torso off the back deck (creating instability) while cockscrewing into the cockpit. Stay low and you're less likely to flip.

6) Not extending the hand out far enough on the outrigger after the second leg is worked into the cockpit. If your hand is not extended out on the paddle shaft you can't brace as well against the paddle float.

7) Not being able to get up on the back of the kayak to initiate entry into the cockpit. Sometimes its the PFD catching on the edge of the kayak. This simply takes practice on coordinating your movements. Smaller people can, while lifting themselves up on the deck, put their first foot on the paddlefloat outrigger to help push up. The problem with this approach is that it tends to rip away the paddle from the hand holding it against the cockpit coaming.

If you are still struggling a key ingredient for success in launching up onto your kayak is using a powerful kick while pushing the kayak downward with your hands. It is important that your hands remain centered over the kayak as you push down so as not to tilt the boat over. So in effect, as you kick powerfully, you are pushing the boat downward, your torso is rising straight upwards out of the water and then you pull your upper body over the back deck.

Still no luck. You might have to work on your upper body strength. Time to hit the gym, eat those Wheaties.

Practice Session:

Spend that time onshore practicing what steps you can. Get the routine down. Then get out in the water. If you have a friend have them spot you, ready to perform a T-rescue if necessary. Don't rush it. Think about each step as you go through your paddlefloat rescue. Eventually you should be able to do this rescue with a blindfold on.

Alternative Self-Rescues

Actually you still have options if you can't master the paddlefloat rescue. I'll list a couple of them starting with the sling paddlefloat rescue.

1) The sling rescue. You can buy or make a sling for this rescue. Essentially you are going to create a stirrup so you can use leg power to help boost yourself up onto the back deck of your kayak. A typical sling might be a 13-15 foot length of one inch wide webbing. Tie it off in a loop. To set your sling up while in the water loop it around one end of your paddle just below the

Left to right. 1. *Loop sling around shaft.* 2. *Place foot in sling stirrup* 3. *Use leg power, launch onto deck.* 4. *Stabilize on backdeck then remove foot from stirrup.*

paddle blade after you blow up your float on the other end. Loop it through itself so you can snug it against the paddle shaft. Now position that end of the paddle across the other side over the back deck just behind your rear coaming. The idea is to let the webbing flow under your kayak. Push the kayak towards the webbing to help it flow under the hull. Once you have it loop it over the shaft on your side. Now put your foot in the stirrup and leverage yourself onto the back deck close to the paddle and the rear coaming. From here you continue your paddlefloat rescue as normal. If the stirrup is too long wrap it around the paddle shaft on your side a few times to take in some slack. This is one approach to using a stirrup for assistance in your self-rescue.

2)   There's a lot of kayaks made these days with a method for trapping the

paddle blade (usually via deck rigging or straps behind the rear coaming) against the deck of the boat. This in effect stabilizes and keeps the outrigger in position. One less thing to worry about and hence you can put more energy into getting your body up on the kayak. Just as in the paddlefloat rescue you'll place your float on one end of the paddle and blow it up firmly. Then run the "free" paddle blade under the deck rigging behind your rear coaming. In this scenario you'll usually need to launch onto the back deck just in front of your paddlefloat outrigger instead of

behind as usual because the paddle is lined up further from the cockpit than normal. The rescue continues now as usual but you'll only place one foot on the outrigger shaft and start working the closest leg into the cockpit. The crux move really is that once you are in the cockpit and all settled you'll have to pull the paddle from under potentially tight deck rigging to use it. Reaching back to do so means you are more vulnerable to flipping as your paddle slides free. Yowza!

If you can't perform the standard rescues with consistency due to physical limitations and need to rely on "alternative rescues" it is critical that you master them. Start off in calm water and eventually practice in more challenging conditions.

64

65

THE T-RESCUE

This is a great rescue for getting another paddler quickly back into their kayak. Most paddlers find this rescue fairly easy to execute. Thank you God! As in the paddlefloat rescue there are variations to this rescue dependent on certain circumstances. But here I'll focus on the typical or classic T-rescue.

As soon as you notice a capsized kayaker, paddle swiftly towards them, aiming for the bow of their kayak. As you approach the rescuee ask them if they are okay and to hold onto their paddle and kayak. Remember, you as the rescuer are in charge. Take control, keep an eye on the rescuee and give clear directions. Assuming they are not overly anxious have them flip their kayak right side up and you should immediately latch onto the front grab loop. This gives you a secure connection to the capsized kayak and the person in the water. You can also use their kayak to brace off of to keep from flipping over as you'll now need to put your paddle aside to free up your hands. As you tuck your paddle under the front deck rigging or slide it up against your stomach and PFD tell the rescuee to make their way to the bow of your kayak. If they are closer to your stern they can go in that direction. The key is to make sure that they maintain a firm grip on their kayak as they pull along it to get to yours. In other words, they should always be connected to the "raft." They should also hang onto their own paddle because you have enough to do as it is. If the rescuee loses connection to the raft and there's a strong wind, chop and or current you've exponentially multiplied your problems.

As the rescuee is moving towards your bow you should be leveraging their kayak into a perpendicular position to yours and start sliding it up and over your cockpit. The rescuee can wrap their arms around your bow and hang out as you continue to pull their kayak across your cockpit. Once the nose of their kayak comes all the way across your boat you can start rotating it upside down. Water will immediately start to drain out.

How far across your boat do you need to pull theirs? Not very far but you can ask the person in the water if their boat looks drained. When in doubt pull it far enough over so that you can touch the front of their cockpit. The best way to do this is to cradle your arms under their kayak, lift it off your cockpit and pull it over. Now lift it up again and flip their boat right side up. Do this quickly so you don't scoop any water back in.

As you slide their kayak back into the water start orienting it so that the two boats are bow to stern and are

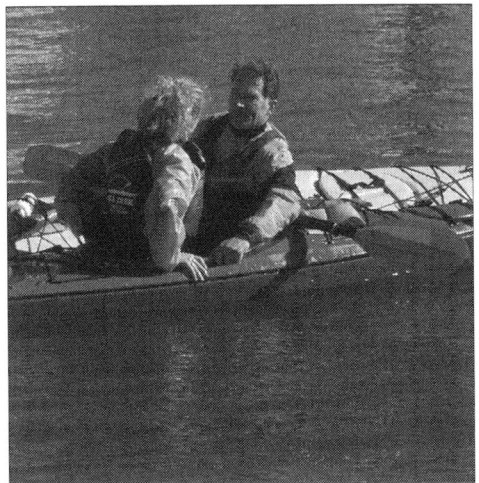

67

parallel to each other. Shift their kayak so that you are positioned next to the front of their coaming. Tell the rescuee to come along the outside of their kayak and position themselves behind their seat. Take their paddle and yours (if it was resting against your stomach) and position the paddles perpendicular to the kayaks lining them up against the front edge of their coaming and on your side against your pfd or stomach. Therefore the paddles stretch across both boats. Reach both arms over the paddles thus helping to trap them against the kayaks. One hand will reach over and firmly grasp the far side of the rescuees coaming and the other hand will grab the side of the coaming closest to your kayak. Now lean over onto their boat. Tell the person in the water to kick up on the back deck very much as they would for the paddle float rescue. They should then keep weight towards your boat as they work their legs into the cockpit and cockscrew into a seated position.

As they start working their skirt on make sure they have boat control (with their feet established on their footpegs and thigh bracing). Assist the rescuee, if necessary, in putting on their sprayskirt but always keep a good grip on their kayak. Hand off their paddle and pull forward towards each others rudders while maintaining a hold on each others kayaks for continued stability. Check each others rudders. Often the cables of a rescued kayak will be crossed or the rudder line has fallen out of its track. At this point your paddles should be lined up ready to paddle. Check to ensure the rescuee is ready to paddle forward before parting.

DOUBLES PADDLE FLOAT SELF-RESCUE

Your knowledge of the paddlefloat rescue for a single can be used for a doubles rescue. Once again there are quite a few different approaches. As in the rescues previously discussed I'll stick to describing a typical and conservative doubles self-rescue.

When you're paddling a double and you capsize it's time to wet exit. Assuming you have more experience than your partner take charge. As they come to the surface make sure they're okay and then have them maintain contact with their paddle and the kayak. If it's rough leave the kayak upside down, put your float on your paddle and blow it up.

Now it's time to flip the kayak right side up. If your partner surfaced on the opposite side of the kayak to your position you'll use the push/pull technique as in the paddlefloat rescue and have them reach over the hull of the boat pulling the rotating side of the kayak to assist you. If they are on the same side as you are

you can both position yourselves at your respective cockpits and use the push/pull method together.

At any rate, now you're ready to assist your partner in getting in. Presuming they know how to use the paddlefloat method hand it over to them. Regardless of whether or not you are on the same side of the kayak as your partner leverage the boat to keep it balanced and give them some coaching and encouragement. Once they're in the kayak your partner should achieve boat control. They'll hand you over the paddle with the float on it while they brace and scull with the other paddle. If the boat is taking on water have them secure their skirt before you begin your rescue.

Now it's your turn. Up and in! If it's calm they can actually start pumping water

out while you're running through your rescue. Rough conditions will dictate that they brace/scull. This will help keep the kayak from flipping in the opposite direction to your float and also help you keep weight on the float. Once you are in, secure your skirt quickly to limit intake of water and take turns pumping and bracing/sculling. If it's calm and you brought along two pumps, always recommended because doubles take on a lot of water, you can both pump. The final steps are similar to the singles rescue. Close off your skirts, secure pumps and the float and away you go.

If for some reason you forgot or lost your float you can use the counterbalance option. Flip your kayak upright. Position yourself on opposite sides of the double. Coach your partner to slide up onto the kayak just behind their seat, and at the same time they should keep their weight leaning away from your side. Meanwhile, you are holding onto the coaming by your position as a counterweight. Your partner enters the cockpit, legs first, just like in the paddle float rescue and corkscrews into a seated position. Their paddle should be accessible for immediate bracing which means they either held it with one hand or had tucked it under the deck rigging in front of their cockpit.

Once in and after establishing boat control (skirt on if rough) your partner will lean the kayak and brace/scull on the opposite side to where you are getting up in the same manner as they did. Once in, it's time for one or both of you to pump water out, depending on conditions. In choppy conditions this counterbalance approach is much more challenging than using the paddlefloat. But give it a try. Someday you may have no choice.

THE DOUBLES T-RESCUE

I'll review this one quickly. If you are paddling a double kayak and need to rescue another double or a single this T-Rescue is similar to performing a T-Rescue from a single. Whoever is the most experienced should take charge. An overturned double will usually take in a lot more water than an overturned single and so its even more important and advantageous to have the paddlers in the water flip it right side up quickly. (Remember, it's much easier to slide a kayak up onto your deck starting with it right-side up. This is especially true for a double.) Once you have a firm grip on the bow toggle get those in the water to the ends of your double. One to the bow one to the stern while they hold onto their paddles. Now slide the double up onto your deck and then begin to rotate it to pour the water out. Next slide it back in the water bow to stern, brace against the double as you do with a single and get your wet paddlers back in their boat. Voila!

EXTRA POINTS

For those of you having fun with mastering the basic rescues and wanting more read on.

The Cowperson Rescue

This one's for the cowboys and cowgirls in the group. After you've done a wet exit, flipped your kayak and checked the usual stuff (rudder, seatback etc.) line up behind the cockpit. Orient your paddle correctly and place it in a similar position as in the paddlefloat rescue but in this case extending it off one side is not necessary. Launch up on the back deck and then swing a leg over the back deck so you can straddle your kayak much like getting up on a horse. Balance now becomes the question because unlike the paddlefloat rescue, where your center of gravity remains low you are now sitting upright. Keep your paddle handy and brace when necessary. Usually you'll find you are sitting on your sprayskirt. Pull it out by the grab loop and drape it over your thigh towards the outside of your leg. Now scoot right up behind your seat back.

Meanwhile, try and keep your feet as deep as possible in the water and even move them in a eggbeater motion to help with stability. Here goes the crux move. Keeping your hands on the paddle shaft slide your hands forward along the coaming (along both sides simultaneously). With arms extended keep your hands locked on the coaming on each side and pull yourself over the seatback and drop your butt quickly into the seat. Keep your legs splayed outside the cockpit and your feet in or close to the water at this point. This is again aimed at keeping weight down low.

71

1. *Launch onto the back deck.* 2. *Straddle the kayak and keep your hands on the paddle.*

Throw a couple low braces if necessary as you drop into the seat. Now work one leg in at a time. If you are tall this can prove challenging, especially if you have a small cockpit. Keep yours hands on your paddle so you can continue to brace but put your first leg into the cockpit by pulling against your shin with the paddle shaft not your hand. Repeat for the second leg, then skirt on, pump water out and paddle off.

If this rescue proves challenging at first or you are practicing it in choppy water you

3. *Drop butt into seat using legs in water to balance.* 4. *Hands on paddle for bracing while you work one leg in at a time.*

can "cheat" by attaching your paddlefloat to your paddle before straddling your kayak. This will make your bracing much easier and allow you to work on coordinating your movements before trying it without the paddle float.

Some Variations on the Paddlefloat Self-rescue

One of the aspects of the self-rescue which takes up time and energy is pumping out the water once you get back in. Here's a couple ways to dump that water out prior to entering the kayak. These examples work better with a lighter fiberglass kayak then the heavier plastic types.

After you've blow up your float make your way to the bow of your kayak. Position yourself so that you are facing the bow. Place the powerface of your paddle blade on your right shoulder with the float side extended alongside and parallel to the edge of the kayak. Place your left hand under the nose of the overturned kayak. Your right hand will pull down on the paddle shaft which

is supported by the float as you simultaneously scissor kick. The idea is to give yourself some lift as you raise via your left hand the bow of the kayak off the water, breaking the seal between the cockpit and the water. You have to coordinate this movement so you hold the boat up long enough for the water to drain out. Now the crux move. As you lower the boat back down you need to rotate/twist it so it lands right side up. If you can pull this off there's no need for pumping once you re-enter your kayak via your paddlefloat or cowperson rescue.

You can also try achieving the same affect by approaching the stern of the kayak and throwing your weight on the overturned stern. Sometimes your arms and upper body weight against the overturned stern is enough to break the seal and lift the bow. Another approach is to straddle the overturned stern. Either way you'll need to rotate the boat upright before it drops back down to the water.

Re-entry and Paddlefloat Roll

Here's another self-rescue for those who haven't mastered the roll but have good boat control and bracing skills. Imagine you are out of your kayak. Attach and blow up your paddlefloat as usual. Now tilt your kayak sideways and slide your legs in and establish boat control (lock in). Sweep your paddle out and away from your kayak with the paddlefloat end extended outwards. As the paddle reaches a point approximately perpendicular to your kayak start pulling down on it as if bracing. This means that as you pull or brace down you're executing a hip snap. The buoyancy

> Tilt kayak sideways and slide in legs. Now you'll probably have to commit to being upside down to completely brace your thighs and connect feet with the footpegs and back with the backrest.

Top to bottom. 1. *Line up paddle while maintaining "locked in" position.*
2. *Sweep paddlefloat out and away from the kayak and start bracing down as you hip snap* . 3. *Keep head low towards the water as you roll up.*

of the paddle float will make it fairly easy to roll your boat upright. Continue to sweep your paddle back past the halfway point and lift your head out of the water only at the very end of this exercise. From here the rest of steps are similar to the standard paddlefloat rescue.

We've covered the standard class rescues and a few extra. Trust me there's more rescues to learn and more variations on the ones discussed if you feel like expanding your repertoire, having options and having some fun. But master the basics first and that means having a solid paddlefloat and T-rescue.

Chapter 5: Storage, Transportation, Launching and Practicing Skills

In this chapter we'll discuss launching techniques and skills practice on the water. But before we do let's take a look at kayak storage, maintenance and transportation. There are so many options we'll just try and give you the general idea on how to deal with these issues.

KAYAK STORAGE

Ideally you'll store your kayak somewhere inside, out of the sun. If left outside at least cover that boat up. Just like for your skin the sun is your kayak's enemy. That slick red gel coat will fade on your prized fiberglass kayak, that plastic from your Tupperware boat will eventually breakdown. A kayak taken care of can last decades. For boats stored outside you'll also want to keep water from collecting inside it whether you put it upside down or have a waterproof cockpit cover in the case of sit-inside kayaks.

If you are bent on hanging your kayak from the garage rafters then the best approach is using "flat" webbing (think seatbelt type material) slung around the hull. If you have a sit-inside kayak with bulkheads this is pretty easy. Run the webbing directly under where the bulkheads are. Thus you'll use two slings. This is where the boat is the stiffest and therefore is unlikely to "oilcan." No bulkheads? Start at the mid-point and go approximately one third to the ends. Run your slings here. More importantly do not hang your boat by the bow and stern grab loops. This can cause sagging especially if the boat is plastic and the storage area is prone to heating up.

If you are using sawhorses or some type of rack system it's best if that set up includes something that will conform to the shape of the hull. For example, you could buy some closed celled foam and shape it to fit your hull and mount that on top of the sawhorses. An outdoor rack with piping for crossbars on which you place a plastic kayak is a good way to get some serious oil canning in your boat's hull. What's happens is that the heat softens the plastic and the weight of the boat comes down on the piping or cross bars. If those cross bars are not directly under the bulkheads or you don't have bulkheads the boat (plastic) will sag or droop around the crossbar. Cool temperatures at night will lock that sag or oilcan shape into place. Hot day time temperatures will only maintain the problem. Eventually the memory of the plastic re-shapes itself into a permanent oil can or dimpled look.

Storing a kayak on a flat even surface indoors or outdoors is another option. Of course, by now you get the idea that a shaded and cool indoor area is the superior option.

You might put something on the softer side between the boat and the ground. The flat surface option is good because it helps distribute the weight and hence you're unlikely to get any oil canning or dimpling.

GENERAL BOAT MAINTENANCE

The ideal scenario means rinsing your kayak off after each use unless you've been paddling in freshwater. Of course, you'll do the same for all your other gear as well. Especially those booties! Naturally water conservation is an issue here.

As implied the rinse off is more important for salt water boaters. In particular, you want to rinse off the salt and grit from foot peg tracks (if you have them), cables, lines, webbing, deck rigging, material made seats, any neoprene hatch covers, rubber gaskets and so forth. Leave your hatch covers open so storage areas can dry out.

CARRYING AND TRANSPORTING YOUR KAYAK

Unless you are lucky enough to live on the water with a boat dock you'll have to deal with moving your kayak to and from your car and to the water's edge. If you have a paddling buddy or someone to assist you these issues are minimized. However, if you are going for a solo paddle (yes we do support the buddy system) you have some things to deal with. And dealing with them has a lot to do with your own physical conditioning.

Can you lift your kayak onto your car's roof rack system? Can you get it down? Can you carry it from your car to the water and back?

First of all let me deal with carrying your kayak to and from the water. Generally, there really isn't a need to do this. There are an infinite number of systems for strapping wheels onto your kayak and rolling your boat to the water. The big question is often what type of terrain are you going to be traversing and hence do you need fatter wheels for sand or will skinnier ones do? Finally, if the water is a long distance from your car can your wheel system be folded up and placed inside a kayak hatch so you don't have to troop back and forth to

All around wheels that do well on hard ground as well as sand.

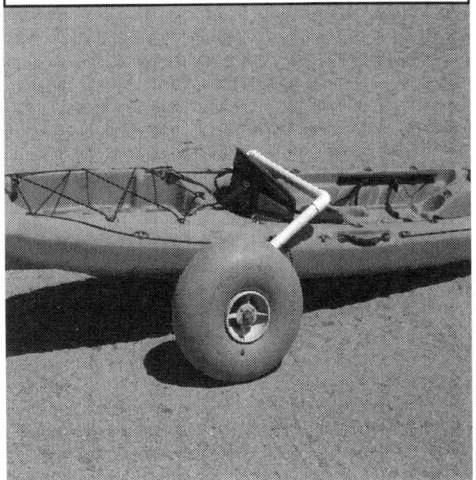

These large round wheels are great for longer stretches of soft sand.

the car.

In terms of actually transporting your kayak on top of your car the important considerations are how to get the boat up onto your rack system and of course what sort of rack system should you have. There are lots of options here and I won't go over them all, however a visit to a store that sells rack systems like Yakama and Thule will address most of your questions. The key is to have an appropriate roof system that is designed to hold kayaks and their weight specs. Many factory made roof racks that come along with that car purchase are inadequate for strapping on kayaks. These manufacturer rack systems usually are rated for load capacities less than a heavy kayak. And of course they don't include saddles to wrap around the hull. When you purchase a rack system that is designed to carry a kayak on your car model proper installation is critical.

Roof rack system: *Crossbars with kayak saddles strapped around a kayak.*	*Here the bow has been lifted onto the kayak saddle.*

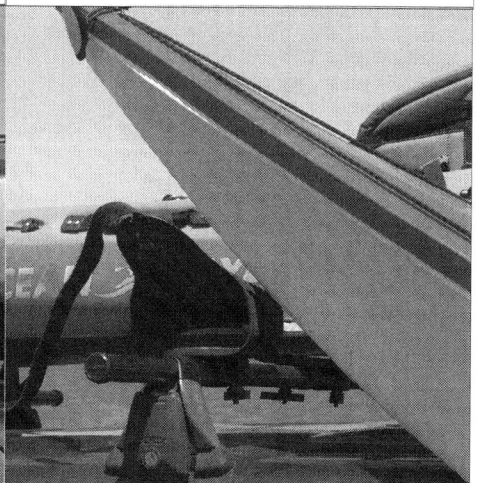

Typically there are two crossbars and the kayak is strapped down to these bars. The crossbars can have add-on specialized kayak saddles, foam blocks or other approaches to securing your kayak. Generally the straps wrap around both ends of the cockpit coaming of a sit-inside kayak or roughly halfway between the midpoint and the bow and stern. Regardless of how bomb proof your specialized rack system is a smart back up system is to always attach a bow and stern line. These lines usually wrap through the grab handles somewhere and run snuggly (don't over tighten) down to secure to something solid under the front and rear car bumpers. If your rack system fails your kayak will not go flying into the driver's windshield behind you.

The difficult task when alone, of course, is getting your kayak up onto your rack system. This is where your physical condition and agility comes into play. Maybe you have the physical ability to hoist your kayak up onto one shoulder, and approaching your car from the rear you slide your boat into the saddles. Many kayakers put what are called rollers on the rear roof crossbar and hence can roll their boat onto the

racks once they place the nose in the rollers. If this is too difficult perhaps you can try lining your kayak up parallel to your car with the bow just overlapping the front crossbar. Now lift the nose up and onto the crossbar. Make sure it doesn't slip off and go to the stern and lift the back of the kayak up and over onto the rear crossbar. Or you can try this approach by lining up your kayak so the nose just overlaps the rear crossbar. Once you get the bow up on the rear crossbar then go to the stern and slide the kayak forward to the front crossbar.

There are also side lift systems where arms extend downwards from your roof racks along the side of the car. In this case you just have to be able to lift your kayak about hip high before slipping it into the lifters.

Whatever method you choose don't strain yourself. Usually there's someone around whose willing to help you. You just have to ask.

LAUNCHING

Ah, finally you're ready to launch. You've read the earlier chapters, you're geared up and have checked out your kayak. As well you've reviewed your strokes and choreographed your basic rescue moves on dry land. Now you are ready to apply all this to the water environment. We'll discuss launching techniques and then getting to work on your paddling strokes, boat control and rescues.

Here we'll discuss calm water launches only. Discussing and practicing surf zone launches, amongst the most challenging launches in the kayaking experience, is best saved for another time.

For calm water launches (no waves) there are a number of considerations, primarily to do with the terrain you're launching from. Is it a sandy or rocky shore, steep entry or shallow or are you launching from a dock? A sandy beach to launch from, in a calm and protected harbor is probably the easiest way to go so we'll start here.

Beach Launch

You have choices. If you want to keep your feet dry, position your kayak so that the front of the seating area is just at the edge of the water.

Sit-on-top kayaks

You can straddle your kayak and drop your butt onto the seatwell and then pull your legs in. This is a tad uncomfortable when you have a wider kayak or you are the shorter limbed version of homo sapien. Another approach is to stand on one side of the seating area, turn your butt towards the kayak and drop it into the seat. As you lower yourself into your seat you'll steady yourself with your arms and hands. For example, from the right side of your kayak your left hand will reach over to the opposite side while your right hand grasps the gunwale closest to you. Once in the seat then swing your legs into position.

Sit- inside kayaks

Stand with your legs on each side of the cockpit. Keep your back straight and perpendicular to the ground, and as you bend your knees have your hands grasp the coaming on both sides. Your hands grasp the coaming at the sides of your hips. Keep your arms straight and then work one leg into the cockpit followed by the other leg. As you drop into your seat your arms will now bend at the elbows as if you are doing a tricep dip exercise. Once in, establish boat control with your feet on the footpegs and seal on your sprayskirt.

Another approach is the same as for the sit-on-top where you stand on one side of the kayak and drop your butt into the seat, pivot frontwards and then pull in your legs. For this maneuver you'll place one hand centered on the front of the coaming and one centered at the rear as you lower yourself down into the seat. This "side-sit" method is challenging to use if you are longer limbed or have a small cockpit.

Sit-on-top & Sit-inside kayaks

Where has your paddle been positioned this whole time? It could have been on the ground next to your kayak,

or one of the paddle blades might have been tucked under the deck rigging in front of you allowing for easy access.

Now you are in your boat but half the kayak is on solid ground. So how do you get in the water from this position? Firstly, if not already take your paddle, orient it correctly and place it close to your stomach so you have quick access to it. Now drop your hands down to the sand and use your knuckles to "chimp walk" as you scoot your kayak forward by pushing off with your knuckles and jerking your body forward (legs pushing into the footwells/footpegs to help drive the boat forward) each time you push off. This technique can be challenging if the entry is very shallow causing a lot of drag until you reach the freedom of deeper water. Those with shorter arms might also find this approach difficult. An alternative to the chimp walk, one however that can chip your paddle, is to hold the paddle like a spear in one hand and use it to push off the sand on one side and use your fist or a stick on the other side.

So the next question you might ask is how important is it to not get my feet wet?

WATER LAUNCH

A water entry is an easier method, in terms of energy expenditure, and less abrasive to the kayak's hull. This is also the version to use with a rocky shoreline or a very, very shallow entry where there are no waves, and the chimp walk would just be too impractical. Walk your kayak out into the water so it is free floating. Ankle deep water will often suffice but you can go a bit deeper if you like.

Sit-on-top kayaks

For a water entry on a sit-on-top it's best to stand on one side of the seatwell and lower your butt into the seat. The key is to try and not tip the boat one way or the other. Position yours hands to keep the kayak stable and make

84

sure you lower your butt directly over the seat as opposed to catching the edge. Now swing your feet into position and paddle off. If you find your kayak "catching" the bottom just a bit take your paddle and use it to help push off being careful not to strike a rock. No luck, get out and start in deeper water.

Sit-inside kayaks

You can basically use the same methods described for getting into sit-insides as when part of the boat is resting on the ground. The key however, since your boat is not being stabilized by the ground is to use proper hand placement to keep your kayak from tipping one way or the other. If you use the straddle method the crux move is when you pull the second leg off the ground and into the boat. The weight on your arms and hands needs to be even as they grasp both sides of the coaming. The "side sit" method also requires keeping your kayak level as you drop your butt in. Remember your hand placement.

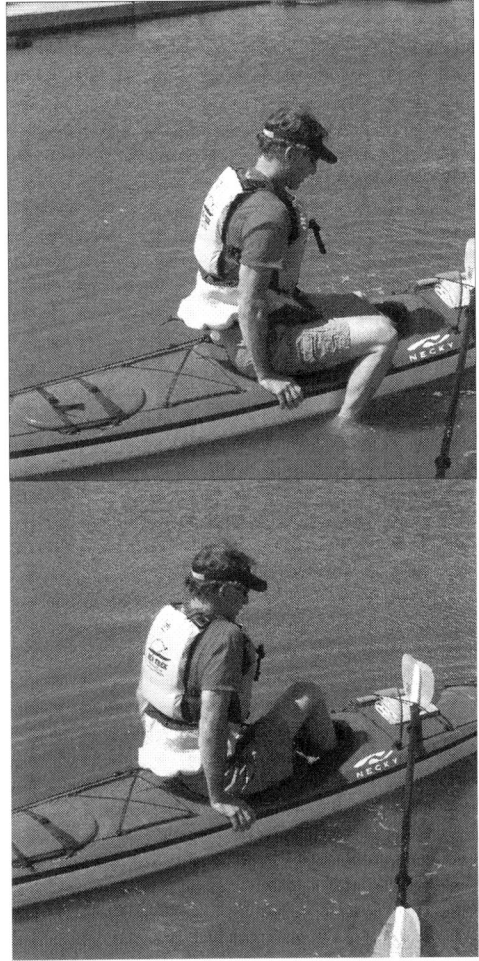

There is another option to getting into your sit-inside kayak in a water launch situation. You can use your paddle for support. Position it, as you would for the paddlefloat rescue with one end of the shaft behind the rear coaming. The backface of the extended blade should rest flat on the ground. For this example, your paddle is extended off the left side of your kayak kept at a perpendicular angle. Your body should be positioned just in front of the extended paddle with your right leg touching the left side of the kayak. Your right hand fingers will wrap around the inside of the center rear coaming while your palm and thumb secure the paddle against the deck and right up against the coamings rear edge. Now bend your knees. Keep your back straight while your weight is

85

supported by your right arm and legs. Reach your left hand out onto the paddle shaft with your palm on top and your thumb wrapped around the front of the shaft and your fingers around the back.

Put minimal weight on your paddle as it rests against the ground but always keep some weight on that side much like in the paddlefloat rescue. If it's easier for you, let your butt sit on the edge of the kayak on top of your paddle shaft. Now work one leg into the cockpit. As you do this your weight is now supported by three contact points:

Your right hand securing the paddle shaft to the rear coaming and against the deck, your left leg in the water against the ground and your left hand reaching out on the paddle shaft. Easy enough?

Now it's time for the crux move. Lift the second leg into the cockpit and quickly slide into your seat. As you do this you'll be relying on two contact points. The one maintained by your left hand and the one by your right hand. Once you're seated, establish boat control, bring your paddle in front of you were you can use it for bracing if necessary, and seal your sprayskirt. This approach is particularly effective for people with long legs or those who simply need the support of their extended paddle.

DOCK LAUNCH

Launching from a dock can be a bit trickier especially the higher the dock is relative to your kayak when it's placed alongside. Usually I'll line my kayak up diagonal to the edge of the dock and holding it from the stern grab loop I will slide it into the water, bow first and then drop in the stern and finally bring the kayak right up against the dock's edge.

Sit-on-top kayaks

Let's say you're getting in from the left side of the kayak. First sit your butt down on the edge of the dock and swing your feet into the footwells. Then take your right hand and position it centered and just behind the seat. You'll push down on the right hand and at the same time the left arm (resting on the dock) to lift your butt and slide it down into the seatwell. During this whole time it's important to keep the majority of your weight (via the left arm) on the dock. If the boat kicks away from you pull it back close to the dock either with your right hand, your legs or a combination of the two. Meanwhile, your paddle should have already been placed within reach on the dock. Once balanced in your boat grab your paddle and you're ready to draw stroke away from the dock and paddle off. Sounds easy huh! Practice makes perfect to figure out this balancing act.

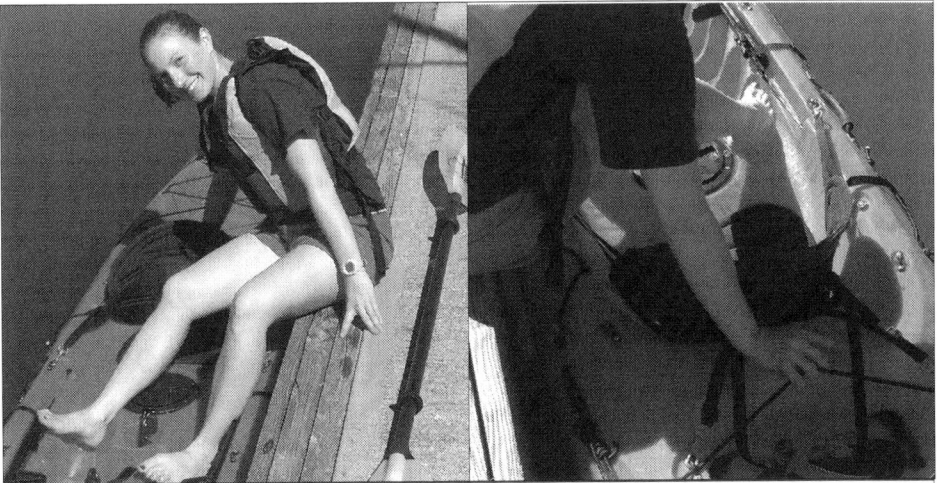

| 1. *Position yourself placing your feet on the kayak.* | 2. *Place your hand behind the seat and centered on your kayak.* |

3. Shift your butt into the seat keeping weight against the dock.

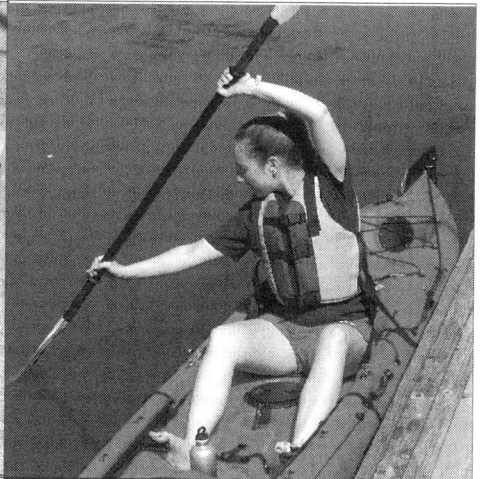

4. Now you're ready to draw stroke away from the dock.

Sit-inside kayaks

Getting in from the left side of the kayak sit your butt down on the edge of the dock and swing your feet into the cockpit, resting them just in front of the seat on the hull. Then your right hand should grasp the center rear coaming. Now putting some weight on your right hand but the majority on the dock side hand and forearm, slide your butt into the cockpit. If the boat kicks away from you pull it back close to the dock either with your right hand, your legs or a combination of the two. Establish boat control, seal off your skirt, grab your paddle and your ready to draw stroke

away from the dock and paddle off.

SKILLS PRACTICE ON THE WATER

Once you paddle away from shore or a dock get comfortable with the primary stability of your kayak. If you have a rudder, leave it up for now so you can focus on maneuvering your boat with paddle strokes.

During these initial forays onto the water its important to always practice your kayaking skills as well as just relaxing and enjoying being on the water. With focused practice sessions your learning curve will be accelerated thus enhancing your experience.

Now that you've spent a few minutes getting a feel for the particular kayak you're paddling go through all your strokes: forward, backward, forward and reverse sweep strokes, the spin maneuver and draw strokes. Refer to the practice session sections in the chapter on paddling strokes to get more ideas.

Your comfort level is up so now it's time to check out the secondary stability (when the kayak's on edge) of your boat. Remember, that by edging your kayak you can turn it faster. In order to put a kayak on edge you need to understand and be able to execute a decent "hip snap." As I mentioned before this is quite practical to do if you are on a sit-on-top kayak that has thigh bracing straps or you are in a sit-inside kayak with good thigh bracing. If your sit-on-top doesn't have thigh straps or your sit-inside kayak has a large cockpit your hip snap won't be very effective. Assuming you have a kayak that allows you to hip snap adequately here's a great exercise to practice this skill before attempting edging.

The Bow Hip Snap Drill

If you have a partner (if not the edge of a dock will work) position your kayak perpendicular to their bow. Your seatwell or cockpit should be positioned adjacent to their bow. Secure your paddle trapping the blade under some bungee cord.

Assuming their boat is perpendicular to the right side of your cockpit, place your right hand and forearm on top of the bow, a couple feet from the nose. Your arm should not be extended, maintain a bent elbow. This will help protect your shoulder joint just as we discussed when bracing. (In fact, you will be bracing against your

partner's kayak, which in effect replaces your paddle.) Your left hand is placed on top of the bow close to the nose of the kayak.

Maintain your hand position and lean your upper chest on top of the bow with one side of your face against the deck. Initially you will stay in this position and just practice hip snapping your kayak over on its edge and then back towards an upright position. Back and forth. This should become very fluid. Leave your chest and cheek resting on your partner's bow. Your arms should be relaxed instead of tense and pushing.

Once you've mastered this you're ready for the next step. Bring yourself completely upright now by hip snapping until your kayak is almost upright then give a little push or brace off your partner's kayak (lift your head last). If you are straining to do this exercise, and are muscling it with your arms you are doing it wrong. Again the head and chest should be the last things to come upright. It is almost as if your upper body is limp like a rag doll. Mostly you hip snap aggressively along with a little push or brace off your partner's boat. If you jerk your head up too fast, this tends to pull the boat back over.

Easy? Need more of a challenge? If not move on to the "edging" section to follow. Get in position and lean over onto your partner's boat again. Hip snap your kayak on edge. Now dip your head in the water, leave it there as you start hip snapping your kayak upright bringing your head up last. An even easier way to recover from this position is to roll your chest and head towards the rear as you come out of the water.

If you don't understand why raising your head up last facilitates getting upright, before you start your hip snap, start jerking your head and body upright first. Feel the difference?

Now do the same thing again but this time take one hand off your partner's kayak so you can sink your body and head deeper into the water (for this exercise I usually hold on to the grab loop with my remaining hand). Now before you begin your hip snap work your other hand back on top of the bow. Two hands on your partners boat equates to better protecting your shoulder joints should you use to much arm pull. Now execute that hip snap with gentle pressure on the kayak following the above steps until you are completely upright.

The final evolution in this series is to dip your upper body even deeper and rotate your kayak via your hip snap completely upside down. Keep in mind that this is much easier done in sit-inside kayaks. In fact, unless your sit-on-top kayak has a rounder hull, is narrower than the average model and has great thigh straps forget this exercise. Of course, you'll need to keep one hand grasping the grab loop or bow of your partner's kayak. Relax a second and then recover back to an upright position. Remember it is critical not to muscle up using your arms. If in fact, you find yourself disoriented or your knees have slipped off your bracing points exit your boat rather than risk injuring your shoulders by muscling this exercise with your arms.

Edging

Keep in mind that you don't have to practice everything mentioned in this chapter during the same paddling session. Maybe at first, you'll just get comfortable in your boat as well as go through your basic strokes. Regardless, at some point you'll want to tune into edging your kayak. Having practiced your hip snap as above it's time to work on edging. Refer to the section on sweep strokes in Chapter Two for combining a sweep stroke with edging.

Bracing Practice

Since you now have a consistent hip snap you can also work on your low brace. You can practice in shallow water as discussed in the practice session of Chapter 2. You'll also want to practice in deeper water as well. You can either have your partner try and tip you over using leverage on your bow or stern or use your own "body english" to partially tip yourself over. Recover with a low brace.

Practicing the high brace is a little more delicate situation as discussed earlier because of the potential for shoulder injury. Again never muscle through this exercise

1. *High brace position, elbows in.* 2. *Brace down in water as you hip snap.* 3. *Lift head last.*

with your arms and always keep your elbows tucked in close to your torso. Here's a few practice options.

Inflate your paddlefloat on one end of your paddle. Position your paddle perpendicular to your kayak, elbows tucked in and tip over towards the float side. The key is to maintain boat control (thighs bracing, feet on footpegs) and keep your paddle perpendicular at all times. Now hip snap upright while bracing down on the paddlefloat. This will help you with timing and also move you towards the next step.

The next step in this evolution of high brace exercises is to do the above without using the paddlefloat. When you can achieve this you'll probably now have mastered the timing and technique used for all the hip snap and bracing exercises discussed.

Using Your Rudder

The First Commandment of using a rudder is know thy rudder system. There are a number of different parts to the typical system.

The rudder is attached via a hinge system to the rudder housing which is attached to the stern of the kayak.

There are steel cables that run from the rudder to the end of the sliding bars to which your footpegs are secured. Therefore the movement of your footpegs turns the rudder. When the rudder is deployed you push your right foot forward and you go right. Left to go left.

The rudder lines found running on top of the kayak deck, from the rudder along one or both sides of the boat, to a position behind the rear of the cockpit, are for lifting and dropping the rudder.

There are usually either one or two cleats in which the rudder line is secured to hold the rudder in the up or down position.

The Second Commandment of using a rudder is check out the rudder system before you leave the beach. Too often I've seen paddlers take off from the beach and once on the water struggle to deploy their rudder. Maybe the rudder line has popped out of its track (back where it attaches to the rudder to pull the rudder up or down). Sometimes the steel cables are crossed over, usually caught on the rudder mount (the device laying on the back deck that secures the rudder when its in an upright position). And then take a look at your rudder lines and practice lifting and dropping the rudder.

When you are ready to practice on the water always make sure you have a couple feet of water under your kayak before dropping the rudder. If you back up with a dropped rudder or get pushed sideways by a boat wake you can easily bend or break your rudder in the shallows against the ground. To drop your rudder, reach behind you and pull the appropriate rudder line to deploy the rudder. Not working? If you checked everything out on the beach then it's probably because one of your rudder lines is still in a cleat. Release all lines from any cleats. Now pull the rudder line forward tightly to secure your rudder in a vertical position, keeping that same line taut (pulling forward) and drop it down and into the cleat. This will keep your rudder in a tight vertical position offering greater turning power. On the other hand if you were paddling along a shoreline and you thought there might be a few submerged rocks but still want use of your rudder leave this same line out of the cleat so the rudder will kick up if it hits anything. Naturally, the best thing to do when in doubt is pull the rudder upright.

Making sure that all lines are out of the cleats pull the other line and your rudder should come up. If your feet are even as you pull that line your rudder should drop right into the rudder mount. Now pull that same rudder line tight and drop it into the cleat to keep your rudder secured in the rudder mount. Practice lifting and dropping your rudder until you can do it without turning around to watch.

Drop your rudder back down and secure it in a vertical position. The ideal use of the rudder calls for slight corrections via your feet. Remember, the more extreme you turn the more drag you create. Nonetheless, your footpegs should be adjusted so your rudder has full range of motion. If you have to really reach with your toes to get full turning power adjust your footpegs to a shorter position. If you can barely slide your footpegs they might be too tight.

Getting into a good forward pace, practice making small turns or corrections. Now try a more extreme turn and you should notice the difference on how it slows your forward speed but accelerates the turn. You can also use the sweep stroke combined with edging to turn even faster if necessary or to assist your rudder on a windy day. But remember, the beauty of the rudder is that it allows you to maintain forward speed with a constant forward stroke as your feet do the correcting. No rudder and on a windy day you'll be executing a lot of sweep strokes to maintain a straight line.

The final commandment in using your rudder is not to use it all the time. Like the purists say, you never know when your rudder system might break. Don't be overly reliant on it. Practice handling/controlling your kayak in different conditions without deploying your rudder.

RESCUE PRACTICE

If you are like most paddlers you'll probably put off practicing your rescues because the idea of flipping your boat on purpose just doesn't make sense. But there comes a time when you can no longer avoid the inevitable. It's time to get wet. Dip your hands in the water and throw a little on your neck just to prepare your body for cooler water unless you're fortunate enough to find yourself practicing in the Caribbean.

Work on your sit-on-top or sit-inside self-rescues to the point you can do them confidently. When you can keep your eyes closed the whole time you've got it down. Try the cowboy rescue (sit-inside kayaks), get the balance, bracing and timing down. If you are solo maybe you can borrow a kayak, flip it over in the water and practice rescuing an imagined partner as much as possible. If you have a paddling partner separate yourself for a little realism and see how quickly you can rescue each other.

94

And remember, as much as you want to believe you can, you can't practice your rescues too much!

EXTRA POINTS

Towing Scenarios

It shouldn't be too long before you start kayaking with a tow rope system that is ready for use. What happens if your paddling partner starts tiring and the wind is picking up? With a tow system you can help them along. Or if you are out paddling and come across a kayaker that needs assistance.

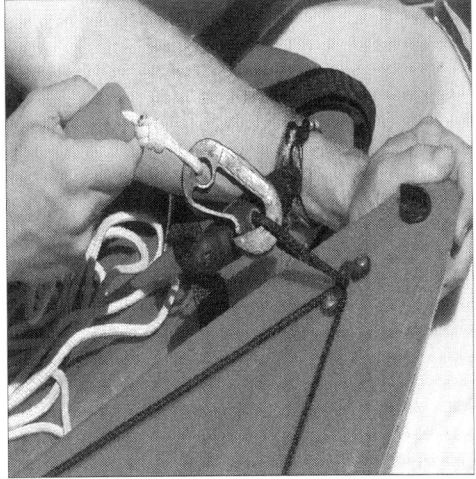

These systems allow you to attach a towline to the bow of another paddler's kayak. There are systems that attach around the waist and those that mount on the rear deck just behind the seat position. And there are many variations. Typically lengths are from 25-50 feet. In flat calm water a shorter tow line is more efficient. In rougher water, in particular with following seas, a longer tow line is needed to avoid collision in case the kayak under tow surf's forward. Some

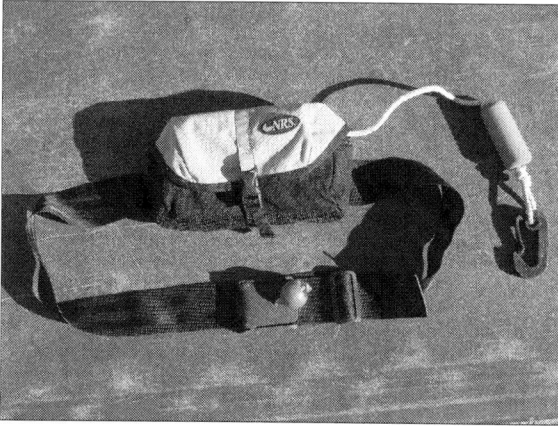

tow systems come with two lengths, a shorter line for quick tows or flat-water situations and a longer tow line for more challenging conditions.

I'll go over a few towing scenarios that you can practice.

If you are towing your partner it's important that they understand their role. Firstly, perhaps to their dismay, they should keep paddling to help you out. Secondly, they need to use their rudder or appropriate strokes to keep the bow of their kayak aimed at your rudder at all times or else they'll be jerking your kayak side to side. Once you start towing pace yourself. If you have a ruddered kayak its not unusual for the tow line to sometimes get snagged under the rudder. To remedy this flip up your rudder, get tension on the line and steer the stern of the kayak away from the line. Then put your rudder back down. You might have to do this several times during your journey. And yes you should use your rudder regardless, if you have one to control your direction.

Practice with a partner by attaching your tow rope to their bow grab loop. See how fast you can deploy your tow rope and begin towing. Get a feeling for the extra physical effort needed for towing.

If there is a third person in your group you can set up an inline tow. Ideally your fastest paddler in front. Their tow line with be attached to the second paddler whose assisting in the tow and in turn their tow line is attached to the paddler who needs the help. In this scenario you have two paddlers helping tow a third. Obviously, this can be a little trickier. Another approach is to do a V-line tow where the two towers are parallel to one another with their tow lines hooked to the third paddler behind. The paddler being towed needs to steer the bow of their kayak in a line between the two towers.

Finally, what if you have a paddler that keeps flipping. Maybe they've completely lost their balance or perhaps they are sea sick. You can only do so many rescues and maybe this person is starting to get quite cold and weak. If you are fortunate enough to have a third member in your party have them raft up against the rescuee for stability. You in turn will hook a tow line onto the rescuee's bow and tow. If there are only two paddlers in this scenario you'll probably have to raft up and try and flag down some help or make a call if you have a VHF or cell phone.

Eskimo Bow Rescue for Sit-inside Kayaks

I'm including this rescue for you to practice at some time in the future. It's not a critical skill to have but if you are one of those paddlers that are really motivated to advance your skills it's a great exercise. The Eskimo bow rescue will give you a greater comfort level with being upside down in your kayak and also help pave the way to a more successful learning curve should you go on to learn the roll. And of course the foundation of this exercise is once again good hip snap technique.

Make sure you have a partner that can control their kayak well. Keep your thighs braced in your kayak and your feet on your footpegs. You can tuck one paddle blade under the front deck rigging and let it flop off the side of your kayak. Flip over, tuck forward and reach your hands around the upturned hull as far as possible. Slap the hull a few times (indicating you need to be rescued) and then slowly sweep your arms back and forth.

Meanwhile, your diligent kayak partner sprints in for a speedy rescue knowing you have a limited air supply. The partner's job is to immediately get the bow of their kayak pushed against your upturned hull where your hands are sweeping back and forth.

Once one of your hands make contact with the bow of your partner's kayak the rest of the exercise is similar to the bow hip snap drill exercise described earlier where you are upside down with only one hand holding your partner's bow. Therefore you need to reach your second hand over to the same side as the hand now grasping your partner's bow. You'll have to figure out the hand placement through trial and error. You know the rest of the drill now. Execute a powerful hip snap and gently brace against your partner's bow with your two hands, rolling your boat upright and lifting your head out of the water last.

Chapter 6: Trip Planning and Safety

It's important to remind yourself that while on the water your safety is generally up to you. Yes, that's right, there's no hovering angel that's going to pluck you out of the water. Kayaking is a self-policing activity and trip planning is an integral part of making good decisions. In this section we'll also discuss related topics such as tides and currents, ranging, and navigational formulas. Finally we'll look at what it takes to progress to the next level.

TRIP PLANNING CHECKLIST

The practice of trip planning covers a lot of territory. Of course, you can do all the trip planning in the world and still get in trouble but you might as well stack the odds in your favor. At least that's how they do it in Las Vegas. Now that you're learning basic kayaking skills and will be getting on the water to practice, trip planning should become routine. For an outlined form of this process see the Trip Planning checklist illustration.

PRE-PADDLE LIST	WEATHER CHECK
Discuss with Group	**Weather Report**
1. General goals	
2. Weather (see box)	**Tides & Currents**
3. Human factors (see box)	1. Low & high tide
4. Communication signals	2. Current speed
Gear Safety Check	**Wind**
1. Pfd	1. Direction
2. Paddle Jacket	2. Strength
3. Sprayskirt	3. Local patterns
4. Paddle	
5. Spare paddle	**Swell**
6. Wetsuit if needed	1. Size of waves
7. Helmet if needed	2. Size of bay chop
8. Paddlefloat & pump	
9. Tow rope	**Other Factors**
10. Food/water	1. Rain
11. Drybag/extra clothes	2. Fog
12. Flashlight (night)	3. Temperature range
13. First Aid	
14. Repair Kit	**HUMAN FACTORS**
15. Tidelog/map	
16. Cell phone/VHF	**Experience Level**
17. Flares, whistle	1. Relative to conditions
Boat Check	**Group Communication**
1. Hatches secure	
2. Deck gear secure	**Physical Abilities/Group**
3. Everything working	1. General condition
	2. Injuries
	3. Seasickness

CONSIDERATIONS ONCE UNDERWAY
En Route Concerns
1. Boat traffic
2. Distance
3. Changing conditions
4. Eddies/rip currents/windbreaks
Landing Places
1. Sandy or rocky
2. Waves
3. Any bailout landing places
Other Factors
1. Group dynamics underway
2. Unexpected injuries
3. Equipment failure

Pre-Paddle List

General Goals:

If you are paddling with other kayakers it's important to discuss the groups general goals. What's your destination? Given the weather conditions and the various skills of the individuals in the group is this realistic? Obviously the above applies as well when you paddle solo. You'll discuss whose the lead and whose the sweep and make sure everyone has checked out their kayaks and has appropriate gear. Other things to discuss are bail out options on the route and any potential hazards like submerged rocks or ships if around boating channels.

Weather Check:

Do some homework before you leave home. Hopefully you have an internet connection. Get familiar with web sites for your area that cover marine and general weather forecasts. Key words to do searches with would be swell report, wind report, tides and currents and your local area name (city, town, body of water). After awhile you'll figure out your favorite sites and bookmark them for easy access. There's also the option of buying an inexpensive weather radio for frequently updated reports. Finally there's the newspaper. Whatever you do it's also very important to get to know localized weather patterns.

For example, perhaps the wind report you've just read has to do with general wind predictions for a very large bay. But maybe you are paddling on a smaller arm of this larger bay in the wind shadow formed by nearby hills. Wind predictions might be 15 knots for the "large" bay with long tracts of open water. At the same time in your very localized area, protected by the hills perhaps the wind is blowing at a very manageable five knots.

Reading the tidelog and becoming familiar with the tides and currents relative to your paddling trip is part of your weather check. A good tide book is an incredibly useful tool if you know how to read it and of course if you are paddling in tidal areas. It can tell you how high or low the tide is going to be so you can avoid, for example, running aground. The tide book also allows you to determine current speed at different times of the day so you know when to avoid strong currents or use them to your benefit. My favorite tide book resource (www.tidelog.com) is called

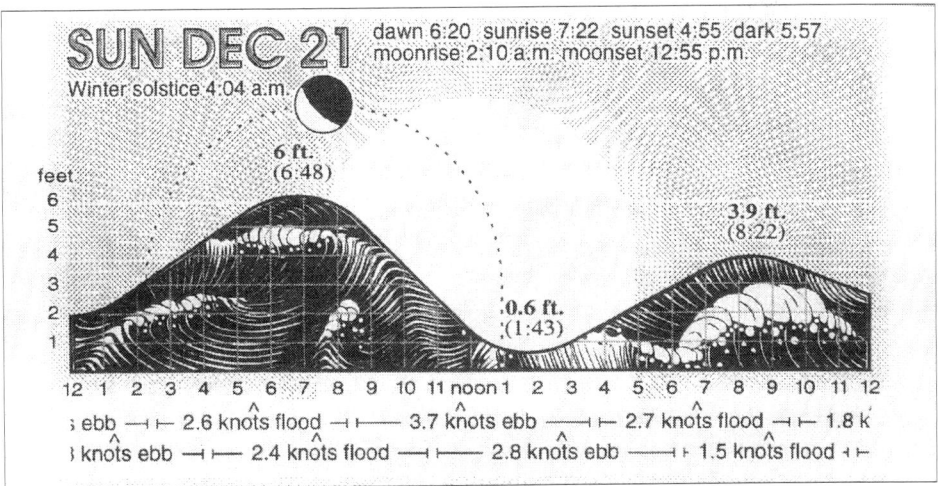

SUN DEC 21

dawn 6:20 sunrise 7:22 sunset 4:55 dark 5:57
moonrise 2:10 a.m. moonset 12:55 p.m.

Winter solstice 4:04 a.m.

6 ft.
(6:48)

feet

3.9 ft.
(8:22)

0.6 ft.
(1:43)

12 1 2 3 4 5 6 7 8 9 10 11 noon 1 2 3 4 5 6 7 8 9 10 11 12

; ebb ⊣ ⊢ 2.6 knots flood ⊣ ⊢── 3.7 knots ebb ──⊣ ⊢ 2.7 knots flood ⊣ ⊢ 1.8 k
} knots ebb ⊣ ⊢── 2.4 knots flood ──⊣ ⊢── 2.8 knots ebb ───⊣ ⊢ 1.5 knots flood ⊣ ⊢

the "Tidelog". Besides covering the above mentioned basics, the Tidelog also does the following; shows you on a weekly basis what planets are visible in the sky, discusses what creates tides, has all kinds of correction tables and includes some cool graphics by M.C. Escher. What a deal!

Here are some of the basic terms and facts. When the tide is going out it is called and ebb tide, and when it's coming in a flood tide. In between the flood and ebb cycle there is always a slack tide. As a friend of mine once said, "slack tide is a state of mind." At a certain point in the tidal cycle, as outgoing and incoming waters counteract each other, there's a point when there's the least amount of movement in the water. This is slack tide. There is still movement but it's minimized.

Each day there are two high and two low tides and these are in between the corresponding slack tides. The flood and ebb cycles each generally last about 6 hours compared to approximately 15 minutes for the slack tide cycle. In the beginning of each cycle, current speed starts out slowly, builds to a maximum current speed and then slows again to reach slack tide.

When referring to current speeds tide books use nautical terminology. For example, a one-knot current means the water is moving one nautical mile per hour. One nautical mile equals 1.15 statute land miles (rounded up). Keep in mind that as a kayaker your average cruising speed is about three knots or 3.45 mph (statute). Of course, this varies widely dependent on your physical conditioning, experience, boat type and weather patterns. However, you probably wouldn't want to be paddling against a three knot current. As they say, you will get nowhere fast and this is simply poor trip planning.

If you continue your paddling experience at some point you'll either purchase a local nautical map of your favorite paddling area or get in the habit of checking out the maps available from your local outfitter. As you decide to explore further, you'll want to get a picture, as part of trip planning, of what to expect. Where are the shallow areas to avoid during low tides, where are the boating channels and so forth?

For the most effective trip planning you'll combine information gleaned from a tide book with information listed on your map. Nautical maps have numbers all over them referring to the depth of the water at Mean Lower Low Tide (average of low tides). These figures are in feet. So during a typical low tide when the tide is at its "average" low point you can see the depth of the water on the map. Using your tide book you can therefore determine whether it makes sense to paddle in a certain

area at a certain time. The tidelog and correction tables will tell us what the current is likely to be. That's what we call the horizontal movement of the water. But there's also vertical movement of water referring to the depth of the water.

Is there enough water? Perhaps your tide book indicates at noon that there's approximately a four-foot tide (meaning four feet higher than the Mean Lower Low Tide). Add this to the numbers you see on the map and you'll get an idea of how deep or shallow certain areas are at that time.

Please note that although you can kayak in two feet of water there is something called "bottom drag" and it'll be slow going. If you want to paddle into the outlying areas of a shallow bay its best to ride the flood tide in when there's plenty of water and paddle back out with the ebb current or at least during slack tide.

Most of all you want to avoid the scenario where you land along the shoreline to eat lunch and stretch your legs, and then get back in your boat only to discover the tide has been dropping and you're stuck in the mud. Pigs are intelligent creatures but...

The wind! Just a few more thoughts on this aspect of the weather. So you checked the weather and with reports of small craft warnings maybe this isn't your day.

What level of wind is acceptable for you? This is something you'll learn with experience but most people who have basic competence and physical strength as paddlers can still enjoy going out in 10 mph (approx. 8.7 knots) winds. In fact, I've been out in 80 mph gusts although I don't recommend this. During the extreme gusts all I could do was lean forward with my boat pointed into the wind and clutch my paddle. In between gusts I would sprint to make headway.

If the wind is starting to blow 12-15 mph (10.5-13 knots) this might not be your day. If the wind is blowing 15 mph and up and you are purposely going out in it you already know you can handle it. If the wind starts bumping up into the low 20s getting closer to small craft advisory you need to be an advanced kayaker with plenty of stamina.

There is a wind chart called the Beaufort Wind Scale. This is simply a chart that relates surface conditions on the water to wind speed to help you judge wind speed. For example, it describes winds running 7-11 mph as having this affect on the water. "A few scattered white-tops. Flag flutters straight out on coastguard station." Here's a description with winds at 22-28 mph. "Rescues will be difficult. Warnings issued to small craft. Seas getting big; white-tops and spray." These descriptions are from Derek Hutchinson's "The Complete Book of Sea Kayaking." You can look the Beaufort chart up online.

Human Factors:
As an adjunct to your pre-paddle briefing you also want to take into considerations the "human factors." What is the mental/physical condition of everyone in your group or if you are solo of yourself. What I mean by this is that gee, Joe has a hangover and only slept one hour last night maybe we shouldn't do that 20 mile crossing especially given the 15 knot winds predicted on the weather channel. Again, be aware of everyone's experience level? Your group member, Maria, has never landed in six-foot surf therefore you probably shouldn't land on that coastal beach with the big dumping waves.

It's also a good idea, especially for larger groups, to assign a group leader, and lead and sweep paddlers to help keep your group together. You should also discuss your route, any related hazards and bail out options.

Communication Signals:
Work out some communication signals amongst the group. There is no absolute standard set of signals amongst kayakers that I am aware of although there is some consensus in regards to the signals I discuss here. The most important thing is that your group has a set of signals and agrees on what they indicate. Along with visual signals it's good to have audible signals where possible so you have several different ways to get your message across.

Vertically raised paddle in the air. This is a signal to gather around the kayaker who is holding the paddle aloft. It is used if some kayakers have paddled to far in front of the group or too far out to the sides. It can be used to group up everyone to communicate whatever is necessary. A single loud whistle can also be used.

Horizontally raised paddle. This is a sign to stop. Two whistles in succession.

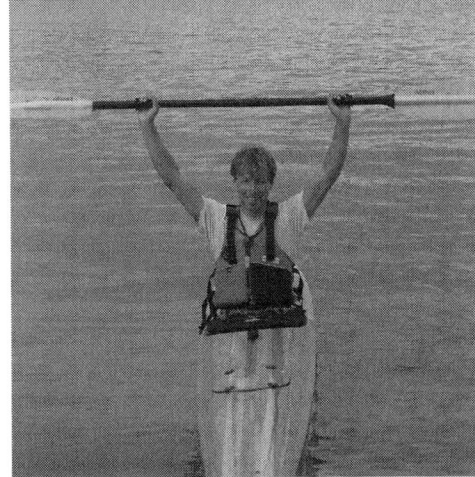

Diagonal paddle pointing in a certain direction. This indicates which way to go. No whistle signals for this one but you can always yell out "go to the right." "Go to the left."

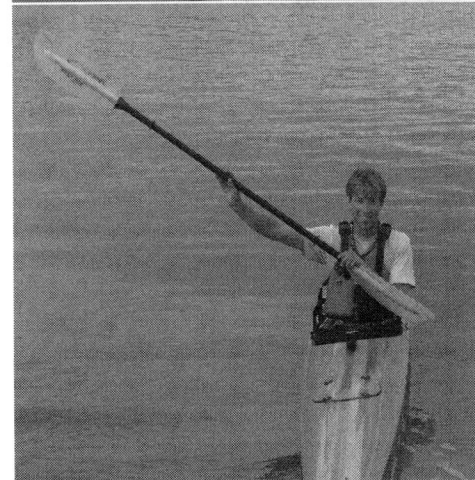

Aggressive back and forth paddle waving. Everyone seems to agree that this signal means you have an emergency. The group should move in quickly to communicate. A series of three or more whistles is the audio signal.

Patting your head. If you want to check in with another kayaker to make sure they are okay, and you can't be heard, pat your head several times. This is like asking, "are you okay?" If they don't pat their head back there's a problem. No whistle signals for this one.

Gear and Boat Safety Checks:

The next chore on your checklist has to do with gear and boat safety checks. In Chapter One I discussed "basic clothing to kayak in" and "outfitting your kayak." This is all part of trip planning--what you do before paddling off. In addition to wearing appropriate layers based on weather conditions (check weather channel), bring some extra layers in a dry bag in case you need to change out of wet clothing or simply require more layers.

To a certain extent the amount of gear you have depends on the type of paddling you are doing as well as weather and sea conditions. If you expect to land/launch through the surf zone (advanced kayakers only) wear a helmet. Wetsuits? As mentioned before there's no argument against dressing for immersion. What if you did flip? How cold is the water, the air and what's the wind chill factor?

At some point you should buy a break- apart spare paddle. This can be secured on the deck behind you. If you did capsize and lost control of your paddle as well as your boat your first action is to try and grab your kayak. This way at the very least you have something to hang onto that will help you float or better yet you can pull yourself out of the water helping to protect against hypothermia. And of course, if you lost your paddle a spare gives you a solution to the problem.

Finally, how can you signal for help if you need it? There are lots of signal devices including everything from signal mirrors, orange smoke canisters, flares, whistles, air horns, VHF radios, cell phones, EPIRBS and PLB's (both location transmitters). A combination of a few of these should do the trick. As a neophyte paddler you're probably not ready to purchase a waterproof VHF marine radio. You could start out with a cell phone and waterproof case, a whistle and some flares for example. Later, you'll workout your ultimate signal kit as well as all the other safety gear you'll want to bring along.

So now that you have your gear together, and your boat set up, including a water bottle and some snack bars in your PFD pocket you're getting ready to go paddling.

Finally all the trip planning you do before paddling off including gear and weather checks amounts to nothing if you don't have your personal radar on when you actually start paddling. In other words keep vigilant. Conditions can change and in some cases quite rapidly. A lot of decisions have to be made on the "spur of the moment." Should I turn back, should I land, can I punch through this rip current? The winds picking up, stronger than predicted? Time to head home.

Emergency gear: First Aid kit, cell phone, VHF radio, whistle and a dry bag with extra clothes.

SAFETY AND JUDGMENT SUMMARY

In this section I'd like to summarize what we've discussed so far and add a few more things to think about. Consider that you now have a trip planning checklist. You know how to prep your boat, personal gear and check out the tide book. Also you have some ideas on what to look for on a map. On top of this you've checked out the weather in terms of wind, water conditions, and is it foggy, raining, hot or cold?

At some point as I already mentioned you'll have an emergency kit. This might include: A First Aid kit, cell phone, VHF radio, whistle, and a dry bag with extra clothes.

There are also those "human factors" to consider. Who's paddling with me?

What is their experience level? Where are we paddling, what is realistic? Discuss your goals. Make them reasonable.

Although some of what goes into a safe and comfortable paddling experience occurs on land before you actually leave, the reality is that a lot of decisions are made on the water. Therefore there are what I call on the Trip Planning Checklist "Considerations Once Underway."

Conditions change and suddenly it's getting rougher or windier. What to do? How are the other paddlers handling conditions? Is someone getting tired? Maybe it's time to turn back? Maybe it's time to land at the nearest spot and find a phone and call for a pick up? Maybe you just have to make a quick decision related to boat traffic.

For example, there's a sailboat or powerboat heading towards us what do we do? In terms of other vessels on the water the rule of good seamanship is to give way. We also jokingly call it the "law of tonnages." They are all bigger than you. Wait and let a boat pass by or make it obvious that you are going to paddle around behind them instead of trying to race across in front of them when the margin of error is slim. And if you are in trouble suck up your pride and signal a passing boat by waving your paddle back and forth, screaming and generally doing whatever you can to demonstrate you need help. They'll get the idea. And finally don't linger or paddle (except to cross) in designated boat channels.

After awhile trip planning becomes, like so many kayaking skills, second nature. Call it a metaphor for life, if you like to get philosophical, but there's no substitute for experience over time. This is your greatest training ground so in the meantime just do your homework as you paddle along and maybe you'll avoid the major pitfalls in your quest for experience.

EXTRA POINTS

Ranging

Ranging is an age-old navigational tool that allows a paddler to determine what adjustments in direction they need to make while crossing to a certain location. The idea behind ranging is to find two stationary objects, one in the foreground and one in the background. For example, if you are making a crossing and intend on landing near a certain point of land you might be interested in knowing whether you are being pushed off course by wind and tides or not. And you will want to know in which direction you need to make corrections to compensate for such factors so that you end where you want.

So on this crossing you pick out that point where you want to land and call this the foreground object. Choose another stationary object behind this such as a lighthouse, a tree, or a building so the two are lined up. As you make your crossing which way does the background object appear to be moving in relation to the foreground object? If it is slipping to the right you are being pushed to the right. To the left and you are being pushed to the left. Let's say it is slipping to the right, therefore you would have to aim the bow of your kayak to the left of the foreground object to compensate. You know that you have chosen the appropriate degree of compensation to the left of the foreground object when these two stationary objects stay in the same relative position as you cross.

Ranging can be more sophisticated than this such as also using a stationary object behind you but basic ranging as practiced above will give you an easy and useful tool.

Navigational Formulas

I'm including some formulas here because kayakers often ask such questions as "how fast am I going" and "how far have I gone?" There are some easy equations to answer these questions. In the end, a greater awareness of the distance you've traveled, the speed at which you paddle and how much time this takes you will help you in planning a comfortable trip.

Basic navigational formulas utilize time, speed and distance. If you know two of these you can figure out the third. In figuring out the below listed formulas, hours are used as whole numbers but minutes are changed into tenths of hours. To convert minutes divide by 60. For example: convert 2 hours 30 minutes. 30 minutes divided by 60 = .5. The conversion therefore is 2.5.

Formula A. Time x Speed = Distance.

Problem # 1. You have time to paddle for 3 hours and 30 minutes. You know your cruising speed is 3 knots (kts). What distance will you cover?

Problem # 2. You take 1 hour 45 minutes to paddle directly to an Island. Your cruising speed is 2.5 knots. You lunch and sunbathe on a beach for 2 hours. Now you decide to circumnavigate the island and then return to your point of origin, all of which takes you 3 hours and 15 minutes. Your cruising speed after lunch drops to 2 knots. What is the total distance you paddled for the day?

Formula B. Distance divided by Time = Speed.

Problem # 3. You paddle from your put in to a bridge in 2 hours 15 minutes. You check the chart on your return and see the distance is 3.5 nautical miles. What was your average speed?

Formula C. Distance divided by Speed = Time.

In the previous examples we divided minutes by 60. In this formula, once we calculate distance divided by speed we must convert the decimal number back to minutes to get our correct time. To do so multiply the decimal number by 60.

Problem # 4. You have paddled 10 nautical miles at 3 knots. How much time did it take?

Answers to the problems.

1. 10.5 nautical miles.

2. 10.88 nautical miles.

3. 1.55 knots.

#4. 3 hours and 20 minutes.

PROGRESSING TO THE NEXT LEVEL-BEYOND CALM WATER PADDLING

How do you get that experience in a sensible manner? There'll be a point in time, probably fairly early in your kayaking experience when some of you start getting the itch to experience more challenging conditions. This section is really for those interested in going beyond calm water paddling. I use the example of progressing through a series of classes to explain ways to progress. If you are a self-taught paddler you'll be able to extrapolate from this suggested progression. Take your time on the road to experience you'll be there soon enough.

Probably the single most important thing to do is practice all your basic skills from launching, paddle strokes and rescues as much as you can during your initial outings. Haven't I said this before? It's simply unsafe to assume that since you did the rescues once in a class or alone (if self-taught) that that's all you need to do. I've had countless experiences with students who sign up for the next level class, say they know their rescues and as it turns out they haven't practiced since their initial class and I end up re-teaching intro level skills instead of bringing them to the next level.

Ask yourself this question. Do I want to trust my life to having only practiced basic rescues once or twice in class? The point is, that the best way to progress to the next level is to master the first level, then move on. Do not be in a rush to "bag" the next class and collect another "certificate of completion."

How much practice do you need? How do you know if you're ready to take things to the next level? These are hard questions to answer yourself and just as hard for an instructor to answer unless they can actually watch you practice to see how you are doing. This topic causes much debate amongst seasoned kayakers. While they argue over exactly when and how to introduce the high brace or the art of rolling you and I will be out paddling. But since neophyte kayakers by definition need some guidance here's my take on "progressing to the next level."

Generally, after an introductory class I recommend that students paddle and practice at least half a dozen times before taking the next class. I say six times a bit reluctantly. It would be best if you played and practiced more but many students are juggling work, family and other priorities in life so it can be challenging to spend more time on the water. If you find you are having a challenge with your basic skills then taking a private lesson can be very beneficial. Also, keep in mind that practice also means building up your paddling endurance so you can comfortably paddle longer distances which is what you'll be doing when you're feeling that "itch."

The biggest problem facing those who kayak and practice on their own is that there is no instructor present to correct bad technique. Something that your fellow kayakers will no doubt help you master. That's the purpose of using this manual so you can learn, remember and review proper kayaking skills.

At this point you are working towards taking a rough water class where you'll do rescues in challenging conditions. The various kayak outfitters usually offer a slightly different series of classes and requirements so you really need to talk to their instructors to check in on how much prep work you need. Just remember a rough water rescue class is a big step up from a basic introductory class. Where I teach kayaking classes you are required to take an Advanced Paddle Class prior to jumping into a rough water class. In the Advanced Paddle Class you will fine-tune the following strokes: forward, reverse, sweep, draw and bracing strokes. You will also work more on boat control via the hip snap and edging, practice your rescues and learn a few new tricks. Here you get further critique and get to solidify all your A-Z introductory kayaking skills.

Once again your instructor, after seeing you in class, can help you determine how much practice you need before advancing to the next level. Remember, that you are working towards kayaking in a rough water environment to experience boat handling and rescues in these more "real" conditions. You should be comfortable with all the skills learned up to this point. What this really means is that you've practiced everything so much you're getting bored. And practice even the basic things like re-adjusting your footpegs on the water, deploying your rudder etc. It's amazing how many people who sign up for a rough water class are awkward at these basic skills including getting in and out of their kayaks.

A rough water class is the next step. What this really means is getting out in chop and current. If you are not in a class environment make sure you have a very experienced support team with you!

As you progress up the ladder of experience and classes, endurance becomes more and more critical. So get out and paddle and push it! Meanwhile, you'll probably start fantasizing about learning the roll (for sit-inside kayaks) and launching your boat off the beach through the surf. Both of these skills require good boat handling and bracing skills, as well as comfort being upside down so work a lot on these things. Your learning curve will be much quicker and you will be less likely to injure yourself.

Some sit-inside kayakers start learning to roll as well as play in the surf zone before bagging their paddlefloat and T-rescues in a rough water setting. That's okay there's different ways to progress but even if you can roll you need to practice the paddlefloat and T-rescues in challenging conditions. For one thing if you miss your roll you are out of your boat and need to know you can get back in when its rough. Sit-on-top paddlers, of course, also need to know how to get back on their kayaks in such conditions.

112

For those learning to roll it will take time to perfect this skill, especially to get to the point where you can roll in challenging conditions. A good way to start is in a heated indoor pool in a river kayak. These small kayaks are easier to roll. Usually you'll need several sessions with an instructor followed by practice on your own or even better with a friend to spot you. Next you graduate to rolling a kayak in calm water and then eventually in choppy water and finally in the surf zone.

So you're starting to think you've arrived! There's a cocky rhythm to your forward stroke, there's a certain panache to your hip snap, and there's the jaunty way your sun hat rides on your head. But suddenly reality hits you when you hear the words "surf zone."

The surf zone. A reality check of sorts. A bit of turf between land and sea to humble the mightiest. Landing and launching in the surf zone off a beach is one of the most intimidating aspects of the kayaking experience whether you are in a sit-inside or a sit-on-top kayak. Imagine you are standing at the waters edge watching the waves explode against the shoreline thinking "I've got to paddle through this?" There's a reason why you're wearing that helmet.

Approach the surf zone with caution, and definitely with that helmet on. It's good to take a surf zone class or two (emphasis here). Afterwards, when you practice try and bring along a more experienced kayaker to help you out (literally and figuratively). Start with small surf conditions; build up your confidence and ability and then go from there. Once you can sit in your kayak, ready to launch with a normal pulse rate through six foot surf you know you've "arrived." You're a rough water kayaker!

Well maybe not quite yet. To paraphrase a quote on the wall in my high school ancient history class, "before the high gates of excellence the gods have placed sweat." Your next goal might be to take an open coast class where you'll be exposed to sea swells, rough water, surf zone kayaking, caving, rock gardens and more. Where does it end?

There's so much more to learn as an advanced kayaker that enhances the experience of being on the water and in short makes you a better paddler. There's learning about: navigation, multi-day kayak trips, rescue and assistance procedures like towing and the list goes on. If you get to this point you will seek out and find the resources, the classes, the experiences and the mentors to enhance your kayaking experience.

Along the way be honest with yourself and your abilities. Know your limits. The majority of today's paddlers are not open coast paddlers. They simply don't have the skill set. There's nothing wrong with sticking to calm water paddling. So how far will you progress? Maybe you don't know yet and that's just fine. In the interim just take your time, move at a sensible pace and enjoy the challenge!

22090824R00068

Printed in Great Britain
by Amazon